Service Matters

The Craft of Exceptional Customer Care

By

Gary Pettigrew

Index

Introduction

As businesses navigate a rapidly changing and increasingly competitive marketplace, it's more critical than ever to provide excellent customer service. Customers expect responsive, personalized service, and are quick to take their business elsewhere when they are dissatisfied. Companies that make customer service a priority are more likely to succeed in today's ever-changing business landscape.

The book aims to provide practical tips and strategies for companies and their representatives to deliver superior customer service to their clients. The ideas and examples in this book are drawn from the most successful companies in various sectors, ranging from small businesses to multinational corporations. Each chapter will be dedicated to a specific aspect of customer service, offering easy-to-understand guidance that can be applied in any company's day-to-day operations. The book is designed to be a must-read for any business looking to improve its bottom line with better customer service.

In this book we will be looking at:

1. **Active listening**: Encourage your employees to listen actively to the customer and understand their needs with empathy.

2. **Patience**: Train your customer service representatives to be patient while dealing with customers, especially when they are in a difficult situation.

3. **Communication skills**: Enhance employees' communication skills

so they can effectively convey information, provide clear instructions, and resolve conflicts.

4. **Positive attitude**: Encourage your team to be positive, upbeat, and courteous to all customers, even if the customer is not polite.

5. **Attention to detail**: Train your employees to pay close attention to details, ensuring that they accurately capture customer information or instructions.

6. **Conflict resolution**: Train your team to identify and familiarize themselves with different styles of conflict resolution to find solutions to satisfy both the customer and the business.

7. **Product and Service Knowledge**: Encourage continuously updating employees with new information about the products and services they serve so they can answer customer questions with confidence.

8. **Time management**: Train your team to be efficient with time and manage customers quickly while still maintaining a good rapport.

9. **Problem-solving**: Demonstrate and encourage employees to have a creative and solution-oriented approach to solve difficult customer problems.

Active listening is an essential customer service training technique that helps employees understand the customer's needs and provide effective solutions. Here are some tips to improve active listening:

1. **Respectful body language**: Train your employees to maintain an open and engaged body posture when the customer speaks to show their interest.

2. **Ask open-ended questions**: Encourage your team to ask questions while customers are explaining their stories to gain more insights and show an interest in the details.

3. **Repeat and paraphrase**: Encourage your employees to restate the key points discussed by the customer to confirm their understanding of the issue.

4. **Empathize and Show Understanding**: Train your employees to show empathy by acknowledging the customer's emotions and showing an understanding of their situation.

5. **Avoid interruptions**: Teach your team not to interrupt the customer when they are talking, as it not only shows disrespect but can also make the customer feel unheard.

6. **Concentrate on facial expressions**: Guide your employees to listen with their entire being, including their eyes, as facial expressions often provide more insight into the conversation's meaning.

7. **Summarize the conversation**: Encourage employees to provide an overview of the conversation, which can help both parties stay on the

same page and increase satisfaction.

8. **Limit Distractions**: Teach your team to eliminate potential auditory or visual disturbances and strive to create a distraction-free setting, so they can listen more attentively.

By improving active listening, your customer service team can significantly enhance customer satisfaction rates and build lasting relationships with them.

Respectful body language is an effective way to show empathy and positive regard to the customer. It helps customers feel that they are being heard and valued during their interactions with your company's representatives.

Below are some tips on how your team can maintain an open and engaged body posture during customer conversations:

1. **Face the customer**: Train your team to face the customer directly, making eye contact and avoiding distractions. This will help them to be more receptive and attentive to the customer's words.

2. **Maintain a natural yet attentive posture**: Encourage your employees to sit or stand with their shoulders relaxed, maintaining an upright but not strained posture, leaning-in slightly indicates interest but avoid appearing overly intense.

3. **Nod and show interest**: Teach your employees to nod their heads, smile, and show interest in the customer's story. This sends a signal to the customer that you are actively listening and encourages them to continue speaking.

4. **Avoid distractions**: Guide your team to eliminate potential noise or visual disturbances, such as answering phone calls, typing on a computer or looking at other customers.

5. **Practice active listening**: Remind employees that active listening is an essential part of showing respect and paying attention to the customer. Avoid preparing responses too early when listening, as this can make customers feel like they haven't been heard.

When your team practices respectful body language, they can establish positive interactions with the customer, create a comfortable atmosphere to exchange information, and hopefully leave the customer more satisfied with their interaction with your company.

Open-ended questions are a powerful tool to elicit valuable information, spark creativity, and promote dialogue. Unlike closed-ended questions that can be answered simply with a yes or no, open-ended questions encourage the respondent to reflect and provide more detailed, insightful answers. In this article, we will explore the benefits of open-ended questions, provide examples, and discuss best practices for utilizing them effectively.

Benefits of Open-Ended Questions

Open-ended questions have numerous benefits, such as:

1. **Encouraging reflection**: Open-ended questions allow the respondent to think more deeply and reflect about the topic at hand. This helps uncover valuable insights that might not have been discovered with a closed-ended question.

2. **Shaping conversation**: Because open-ended questions encourage more detailed answers, they can shape the direction of the conversation in a meaningful way. They allow two people to have a more engaging and fulfilling dialogue, where both parties are able to share and learn.

3. **Encouraging active listening**: When asking someone an open-ended question, it is important to really listen to their response. This helps build rapport and trust between individuals. Active listening is an essential skill to develop when trying to build relationships.

4. **Stimulating creativity**: Open-ended questions can help people think outside the box and come up with creative solutions to problems. By challenging the respondent to think about a situation in a new light, they may discover inventive solutions.

Examples of Open-Ended Questions

Here are some examples of open-ended questions that can help shape a conversation and elicit useful information:

1. What was your favorite part about your job?

2. Can you tell me more about what's been on your mind lately?

3. What was your experience like traveling abroad?

4. Can you walk me through how you make difficult decisions?

5. What would you like to achieve in the next year?

Best Practices for Using Open-Ended Questions

Here are some tips for using open-ended questions effectively:

1. **Frame the question positively**: Avoid passive or negative phrasing when asking open-ended questions. This can set an unproductive tone that is not conducive to sharing valuable information.

2. **Listen actively**: When asking open-ended questions, it's important to listen to the response carefully, express interest, and maintain eye contact.

3. **Avoid assuming an answer**: Keep an open mind when asking open-ended questions. Encourage the respondent to offer their perspective, even if it may differ from your own.

4. **Use open-ended questions in a variety of settings:** Open-ended questions are valuable in many settings, from job interviews to casual conversations with friends. Incorporating them into your interactions can help foster deeper, more meaningful connections.

In conclusion, open-ended questions are a powerful tool for eliciting valuable information, promoting creative thinking, and encouraging positive conversation. By using open-ended questions effectively, you can unlock new insights and deepen your relationships with others.

When it comes to effective communication, repeating and paraphrasing are two important techniques to ensure that the message has been received and understood. The ability to listen and then repeat or paraphrase what was said helps to clarify misunderstandings and maintain a positive dialogue in any situation. In this article, we will discuss repeat and paraphrase techniques and how to use them for better communication.

Repeat Technique

The repeat technique involves saying the exact words of the speaker back to them. This can be useful to confirm that you have heard and understood what was said. Repeating the speaker's words can also be a way to show that you are actively listening and engaged in the conversation. However, it is essential to use this technique sparingly, as repeating everything that was said can be seen as unproductive or redundant.

Paraphrase Technique

The paraphrase technique involves rephrasing what the speaker said in your own words. This technique is useful when the speaker may have been unclear, or you need to confirm that you have understood what was said. Unlike the repeat technique, paraphrasing allows you to put what was said into context and give feedback to the speaker.

Example of Repeat and Paraphrase

Let's imagine a hypothetical scenario where a manager is communicating with their employee about completing a project:

Manager: "I need you to finalize the report by tomorrow."

Employee: "Okay, finalize the report by tomorrow."

This is an example of the repeat technique. Although it acknowledges that the employee understood the manager's instructions, it may appear robotic and insincere.

Manager: "I need you to finalize the report by tomorrow."

Employee: "Alright, let me make sure I understand what you want me to do. You need me to finish up the report and have it ready by the end of the day tomorrow, is that right?"

This is an example of the paraphrase technique. The employee reassures the manager that they have heard and understood the instructions. Additionally, they have provided specific details of the project, which allows the manager to be more confident that the employee has correctly understood the task.

Best Practices for Repeat and Paraphrase

1. Listen actively: Effective use of repeat and paraphrase techniques requires active listening. By staying attentive to the speaker's words, you will be in a better position to repeat or paraphrase their words accurately.

2. Use the appropriate technique: Both techniques have their appropriate use, and it is essential to understand when to use each one. The repeat technique is useful to confirm something that you may have missed, while paraphrasing is more effective to clarify something that was poorly explained.

3. Use the appropriate tone: When repeating or paraphrasing, it is essential to use a tone that matches the conversation's context. A robotic or sarcastic tone will likely not be productive or positively received.

Conclusion

Repeat and paraphrase techniques are effective tools for maintaining a positive and effective dialogue in any situation. Using these techniques can help to clarify misunderstandings and ensure that the message has been received and understood. By using these techniques actively and appropriately, you can improve your communication skills and build better relationships with others.

In a customer service environment, empathizing and showing understanding are two essential skills that can make a huge difference in building a positive relationship. It is important for customer service representatives to put themselves in the customer's shoes and show empathy for their concerns. In this article, we will discuss the importance of empathy and understanding in customer service, how to demonstrate them, and how to build effective customer relationships.

Why Empathy and Understanding are Important in Customer Service

Empathy and understanding are important in customer service for several reasons. Firstly, it helps build trust between the customer and the representative. Customers want to feel heard, understood, and valued. When a customer service representative demonstrates empathy and understanding, it shows the customer that the representative cares about their needs and wants to resolve their problem.

Secondly, empathy and understanding can help the representative diagnose the customer's problem quickly and effectively. By understanding the customer's situation, the representative can provide a more efficient solution, reducing the time and effort required to resolve the issue.

Lastly, demonstrating empathy and understanding can help build a positive reputation for the company. Customers are more likely to remember and recommend a company that made them feel heard and understood. It can help to establish a loyal customer base and improve the company's reputation.

How to Demonstrate Empathy and Understanding

There are several strategies that customer service representatives can use to demonstrate empathy and understanding:

1. **Listen actively:** To show empathy and understanding, it is essential to listen actively. This means paying attention to the customer's words and asking questions to clarify their problem.

2. **Use empathy statements**: Use phrases such as "I understand how you feel," "I can imagine how frustrating that must be," or "I'm sorry to hear that." Using these statements can help demonstrate empathy and show that you care.

3. **Paraphrase**: Repeat what the customer has said in your own words to show that you understand their problem fully. It also helps to avoid misunderstandings.

4. **Offer solutions**: Once you understand the customer's problem, offer solutions that meet their needs. You can ask them which option they prefer, giving them more control over the situation.

Building Effective Customer Relationships

Demonstrating empathy and understanding can help to build effective customer relationships. Here are some tips for building strong customer relationships:

1. **Be consistent**: Consistency is key when it comes to customer service. Ensure that each customer is treated with the same level of care and attention.

2. **Follow-up**: Following up with customers after the issue has been resolved can help to build a stronger relationship. It shows that you care about their experience and want to ensure that they are satisfied.

3. **Show appreciation**: Expressing gratitude for a customer's loyalty can help to build stronger relationships. Simple gestures such as thanking a customer for their business can go a long way in building a strong relationship.

In conclusion, demonstrating empathy and understanding is crucial in a customer service environment. It helps build trust, diagnose problems effectively, and improve the company's reputation. By listening actively, using empathy statements, offering solutions and building effective relationships, customer service representatives can make a positive impact on their

company's success.

In a customer service environment, it is critical to avoid interruptions when speaking to a customer. Interruptions can cause frustration and irritation, leading to a negative customer experience. Additionally, interruptions can disrupt the flow of the conversation, making it challenging to understand and resolve the customer's problem. In this article, we will discuss the importance of avoiding interruptions, the common causes of interruptions, and strategies to prevent them.

Why is it Important to Avoid Interruptions?

Avoiding interruptions is crucial in a customer service environment for several reasons. Firstly, it shows that the representative values the customer's time and cares about their opinion. It demonstrates that the customer is being heard and respected.

Secondly, avoiding interruptions helps to maintain the flow of the conversation. This ensures that the customer's problem is understood and addressed effectively. Interruptions can cause confusion and misunderstandings, leading to an unsatisfactory resolution.

Lastly, avoiding interruptions can help to build trust between the customer and the representative. Customers want to feel heard, and interruptions can make them feel undervalued and unimportant. This can damage the relationship between the customer and the company.

Common Causes of Interruptions

There are several common causes of interruptions in a customer service environment. These include:

1. A lack of active listening: Active listening is crucial in customer service. If the representative is not listening carefully, they may miss important details or jump to conclusions, leading to interruptions.

2. Over-eagerness to address the customer's problem: Representatives may sometimes be too eager to address the customer's problem, leading to interruptions. This can make the customer feel undervalued and rushed.

3. Technical problems with communication devices: Interruptions can also occur due to technical problems with communication devices. For example, poor call quality or dropped calls can cause interruptions and miscommunication.

How to Prevent Interruptions

There are several strategies that customer service representatives can use to prevent interruptions:

1. **Listen actively**: Active listening is essential in preventing interruptions. Representatives should listen carefully to the customer's problem and ask questions to clarify any misunderstandings.

2. **Let the customer finish speaking**: It is important to let the customer finish speaking before responding. This shows that the representative values the customer's time and opinion.

3. **Take notes:** Taking notes allows the representative to follow the conversation more effectively, reducing the likelihood of interruptions.

4. **Speak politely and calmly**: Speaking politely and calmly can help to build trust and confidence in the customer. Interrupting or speaking in a rushed or aggressive tone can make the customer feel undervalued.

5. **Check for understanding:** After the customer has explained their problem, it is important to confirm that you have understood it correctly. This helps to avoid misunderstandings and interruptions.

Conclusion

Avoiding interruptions is crucial in a customer service environment, as it ensures that the customer is heard and respected, maintains the flow of the conversation, and builds trust between the customer and the representative.

Active listening, letting the customer finish speaking, taking notes, speaking politely and calmly, and checking for understanding are strategies that can help to prevent interruptions. By avoiding interruptions, customer service representatives can provide a positive customer experience and build strong relationships with their customers.

In a customer facing environment, proper communication skills are essential to establish and maintain successful relationships with customers. Although spoken words are important, facial expressions are also critical in conveying meaning and building a positive impression. In this article, we will discuss the importance of concentrating on facial expressions while dealing with customers, the benefits of using facial expressions, and how to use them effectively.

The Importance of Concentrating on Facial Expressions

Facial expressions are particularly important in customer-facing environments because they contribute to conveying a positive or negative image of your company. Often, customers can observe subtle facial expressions and interpret them as signs of likeability, warmth, indifference, or stress. Therefore, it is important to pay close attention to the facial expressions of the customer and the representative to ensure that messages are being communicated effectively.

Benefits of Using Facial Expressions in Customer Interaction

Facial expressions offer several benefits in customer interactions:

1. **Demonstrating interest**: By using appropriate facial expressions such as smiling, nodding, and raising eyebrows, the representative can convey interest in the customer's needs.

2. **Building rapport**: Smiling and using friendly expressions can help to set the right rapport, making customers feel comfortable and relaxed.

3. **Supporting message clarity**: A smiling face explains more than a thousand words. The use of friendly facial expressions can help in conveying the meaning of the message more clearly and accurately.

4. **Demonstrating competence:** A firm, confident expression, eye contact, and good posture can be signs of competence, reassuring customers that they are in safe hands.

How to Use Facial Expressions Effectively

The use of facial expressions can be a useful tool in customer interactions. However, it is important to remember to maintain authenticity to offer credible interactions. Below are some tips that should be considered for using facial expressions effectively:

1. **Don't fake it:** While maintaining a friendly face is important, it is equally essential to be authentic. Customers can easily spot if a smile is inauthentic, which can create a negative impression.

2. **Match the message**: Facial expressions should match the message being conveyed. For instance, a serious message should be supported by the appropriate facial expressions to demonstrate the significance of the message.

3. **Avoid excessive expression use**: Facial expressions should be controlled and limited to demonstrate authenticity, as excessive expressions can create a negative impression.

4. **Always look engaged**: Maintaining eye contact demonstrates the interest of the representative in what the customer is saying.

5. **Smile**: A sincere smile goes a long way in establishing trust and demonstrating friendliness.

Conclusion

In conclusion, concentration on facial expressions in a customer facing environment is important. Facial expressions convey meaning and demonstrate the intentions of the representative. By using friendly, balanced expressions that support the message, representatives can establish rapport, build trust and demonstrate competence. It is equally important to be authentic in the use of facial expression. Smiling, making eye contact and demonstrating interest and sincerity can help create positive customer interactions and experiences. Therefore, it is important for representatives to maintain concentration on facial expression when dealing with customers in any customer-facing environment.

Summarize the conversation

In a customer service environment, summarizing the conversation is a crucial step in ensuring that the customer's needs are met satisfactorily. Summarizing the conversation involves restating the customer's issue and confirming the agreed-upon solution. It is an essential tool for ensuring effective communication between the customer and the representative. In this article, we will discuss the importance of summarizing the conversation, the benefits of using it, and how to do it effectively.

The Importance of Summarizing the Conversation

Summarizing the conversation is important in a customer service environment because it ensures that all parties are on the same page. It helps to create clarity, avoid misunderstandings, and ensures that the customer's issue is correctly identified and resolved. By summarizing the conversation, representatives can show customers that they have been actively listening and that their concerns have been understood. Furthermore, it also helps to prevent confusion caused by language barriers or complex issues.

Benefits of Using Summarization in Customer Service Interactions

The use of summarization in customer service interaction offers several benefits:

1. **Clarity**: Summarizing the conversation provides clarity to both the representative and the customer, ensuring that everyone understands each other's perspective.

2. **Confirmation**: Summarization allows the representative to confirm that they have correctly understood the customer's issue and that the agreed-upon solution is acceptable.

3. **Improved customer satisfaction**: Summarizing the conversation demonstrates that the representative is taking the customer's needs seriously and is committed to resolving their issue. This, in turn, increases customer satisfaction.

4. **Efficiency**: By identifying the issue quickly, summarizing the conversation helps to avoid unnecessary discussions or solutions that do not solve the customer's problem.

How to Summarize the Conversation Effectively

Summarizing the conversation effectively is essential in ensuring that the customer's needs are met and the issue is resolved. To do it effectively, the following strategies should be considered:

1. **Listen actively**: Active listening includes paying attention to the customer's words, intent, and tone during the conversation.

2. **Break down complex conversations:** Complex conversations can be challenging to summarize effectively. It is essential to break down complex conversations into smaller and more manageable parts to ensure accurate and effective summarization.

3. **Use active language**: Use active language like "I understand that..." and "What I'm hearing you say is..." to confirm the understanding of the customer.

4. **Emphasize the agreement and solution**: Summarization should emphasize the solution that has been agreed upon, so there is no confusion.

5. **Seek confirmation**: It is important to seek confirmation from the customer that the summary made was useful and accurately summarized their needs and that the agreed-upon solution was acceptable.

Conclusion

In conclusion, summarizing the conversation is an essential tool in any customer service environment. It is a valuable method for establishing effective communication, ensuring clarity and accuracy, confirming agreements, and improving customer satisfaction. By summarizing the conversation, representatives can satisfy the customer's needs and create a positive customer experience. They should listen actively, break down complex conversations, use active language, emphasize agreement and solution, and seek confirmation to ensure effective and accurate summarization. Thus, using proper summarization techniques can provide a pathway for effective communication and better customer service.

Limiting distractions during customer interactions is critical to ensure successful communication and build strong relationships with customers. Distractions can occur in a variety of ways, including interruptions, multitasking or background noise. When dealing with customers, representatives must limit distractions to ensure that they can effectively address their needs and provide the best possible service. In this article, we will discuss why limiting distractions when speaking to customers is essential, what kind of distractions can be present, and how to limit those distractions.

Why Limiting Distractions is Essential

Limiting distractions when speaking to customers is essential because it helps to create a professional and attentive environment. Distractions can significantly impact the quality of the communication, causing misunderstandings and frustration for the customer. By limiting distractions, it helps to ensure that the representative is listening and fully engaged in the conversation. This, in turn, builds a positive reputation for the company and enhances the customer's overall satisfaction.

What Kind of Distractions Can Be Present?

Distractions can come in various ways during customer interactions. Some of the most common distractions include:

1. **Interruptions**: Interruptions can be a significant distraction. For example, when the phone rings in the middle of a conversation or when a coworker walks in and interrupts the conversation.

2. **Multitasking**: Multitasking can also be a significant distraction. When the representative is working on something else while speaking to the customer, it can create a lack of attention and decrease the quality of communication.

3. **Background Noise**: Background noise can impact the quality of the conversation. A noisy environment like a busy street, construction noise can make it challenging for the representative to hear what the customer is saying, and vice versa.

How to Limit Distractions

To limit distractions when speaking to customers, representatives can use the following techniques:

1. **Close your door:** Close your office door or move to a quieter location while communicating with customers.

2. **Prioritize**: When you're on the phone with customers, prioritize their needs over other tasks. Avoid multitasking, as it can impact the quality of the communication.

3. **Control the environment**: Try and control the environment so that it is free from distractions. If the setting is too noisy, try and find a quieter environment.

4. **Be Present**: Be present and actively engage in the conversation with full attention.

5. **Use Active Listening**: Demonstrate active listening by asking relevant questions and paraphrasing what the customer has said.

Conclusion

In conclusion, limiting distractions during customer interactions is essential for effective communication and building strong relationships. When representatives limit distractions, they improve communication by ensuring clarity, increasing customer satisfaction, and building a positive reputation for the company. Representatives should avoid distractions like interruptions, multitasking and background noise. They can limit distractions by closing the door, prioritizing the customer's needs, controlling the environment, being present, and active listening. By implementing these strategies, organizations can build loyalty, increase customer satisfaction, and promote a positive company culture.

Part 2 – Have patience

Patience is one of the essential skills required when working with customers. It is essential to remain calm, attentive, and patient, especially when dealing with customers who might be upset or frustrated. Patience helps to build trust and respect between the customer and the representative, leading to better communication and positive customer experiences. In this article, we will discuss some tips on cultivating patience when working with customers.

1. Control Your Emotions

Controlling emotions is the first step to cultivate patience when dealing with customers. Representatives must remain calm, composed and not let their emotions affect their behavior. By exercising restraint and composure, representatives can gain the customer's trust, respect, and confidence in their ability to handle the situation professionally.

2. Listen Carefully

Active listening is a critical part of cultivating patience when working with customers. Representatives should listen to the customer's issues, complaints and concerns carefully. This not only shows respect for the customer but also helps the representative to fully understand the issue, and thus, find an appropriate solution. By actively listening, representatives can provide customers with the attention they deserve and save time in resolving the issue faster.

3. Empathize with Customers

By putting themselves in the customer's shoes and experiencing the issue from their perspective, representatives can understand their situation and empathize with them. This helps to build a connection between the representative and the customer, leading to better communication and finding more effective solutions to the issues.

4. Take a Break

Sometimes, customers may present difficult situations which may lead to frustration for the representative. In such cases, it is important to take a breather, step back, and collect oneself. By taking a break and coming back to the problem with a clear mind, the representative can listen to the customer without any emotional bias and provide an effective solution.

5. **Set Expectations**

In some cases, representatives may have to explain policies or restrictions to customers, which may lead to misunderstandings and frustration. In such cases, setting clear expectations can help to defuse the situation. This can prevent confusion, set boundaries and provide clarity to the customer, resulting in a more positive customer experience.

Cultivating patience when working with customers is a vital aspect of providing excellent customer service. By controlling emotions, active listening, empathizing with the customer, taking breaks, and setting expectations, representatives can provide a proactive approach, defuse potential conflicts, and manage customer expectations. Patience helps to create trust, respect, and loyalty with customers, which can result in long-term positive customer relationships, improved productivity, and overall success for the business.

Patience is one of the essential skills required when working with customers. It is essential to remain calm, attentive, and patient, especially when dealing with customers who might be upset or frustrated. Patience helps to build trust and respect between the customer and the representative, leading to better communication and positive customer experiences. In this article, we will discuss some tips on cultivating patience when working with customers.

1. Control Your Emotions

Controlling emotions is the first step to cultivate patience when dealing with customers. Representatives must remain calm, composed and not let their emotions affect their behavior. By exercising restraint and composure, representatives can gain the customer's trust, respect, and confidence in their ability to handle the situation professionally.

2. Listen Carefully

Active listening is a critical part of cultivating patience when working with customers. Representatives should listen to the customer's issues, complaints and concerns carefully. This not only shows respect for the customer but also helps the representative to fully understand the issue, and thus, find an appropriate solution. By actively listening, representatives can provide customers with the attention they deserve and save time in resolving the issue faster.

3. Empathize with Customers

By putting themselves in the customer's shoes and experiencing the issue from their perspective, representatives can understand their situation and empathize with them. This helps to build a connection between the representative and the customer, leading to better communication and finding more effective solutions to the issues.

4. Take a Break

Sometimes, customers may present difficult situations which may lead to frustration for the representative. In such cases, it is important to take a breather, step back, and collect oneself. By taking a break and coming back to the problem with a clear mind, the representative can listen to the customer without any emotional bias and provide an effective solution.

5. Set Expectations

In some cases, representatives may have to explain policies or restrictions to customers, which may lead to misunderstandings and frustration. In such cases, setting clear expectations can help to defuse the situation. This can prevent confusion, set boundaries and provide clarity to the customer, resulting in a more positive customer experience.

Conclusion

Cultivating patience when working with customers is a vital aspect of providing excellent customer service. By controlling emotions, active listening, empathizing with the customer, taking breaks, and setting expectations, representatives can provide a proactive approach, defuse potential conflicts, and manage customer expectations. Patience helps to create trust, respect, and loyalty with customers, which can result in long-term positive customer relationships, improved productivity, and overall success for the business.

Controlling emotions is an essential part of providing excellent customer service. Representatives must remain professional and composed when dealing with customers, even when the customer is angry or upset. Customers can be unpredictable and sometimes difficult. Hence, it's essential to understand how to handle emotions and understand how they affect customer satisfaction. In this article, we will discuss why emotional control is important, how to control emotions when dealing with customers, and the benefits it provides.

Why Emotional Control is Important

Emotional control is important for several reasons, including:

> 1. **Professionalism:** By controlling emotions, representatives can maintain a professional demeanor and maintain a sense of respect in the eyes of the customer.
>
> 2. **Empathy**: By understanding the customer's perspective, representatives can empathize with them, which helps to build trust and rapport.
>
> 3. **Conflict Mitigation:** Controlling emotions can help to mitigate any potential conflicts that might arise when dealing with difficult

customers, which can make for a smoother and more efficient interaction.

How to Control Emotions When Dealing with Customers

Controlling emotions is essential when dealing with customers. Here are several ways in which representatives can maintain emotional control:

1. **Take a deep breath:** Taking a deep breath is an effective way to calm down and remain focused on the task at hand, especially before engaging with an upset customer.

2. **Pay attention**: Pay close attention to the customer's concerns and actively listen. This will help the representative to formulate a response without becoming defensive or dismissive.

3. **Acknowledge the customer's emotions**: It's important to acknowledge the customer's emotions and assure them that their concerns are being understood and addressed.

4. **Take a break**: If necessary, take a break to regroup and collect thoughts to ensure that interactions with the customer remain positive and productive.

5. **Provide solutions:** Provide solutions to the customer's issue systematically, as this will help to move the conversation forward in a more constructive and positive manner.

Benefits of Emotional Control

There are several benefits to controlling emotions when dealing with customers. These benefits include:

1. **Increased customer satisfaction**: By maintaining a professional and empathetic demeanor, representatives will increase customer satisfaction, which ultimately leads to higher customer loyalty and retention.

2. **Improved teamwork**: Colleagues emulate the behavior of their representatives. By demonstrating successful emotional control, they can model this behavior for their colleagues, which can lead to a better team dynamic.

3. **Company image**: Controlling emotions reflects positively on the company's overall image, enhancing its reputation and resulting in recurring business with that particular customer.

Conclusion

In conclusion, emotional control is essential when dealing with customers. Representatives must remain calm and professional, maintain empathy, and remain focused on reaching the desired outcome. By demonstrating emotional control, the representative can ensure that the interaction remains positive, constructive, and productive, which contributes to overall customer satisfaction and leads to business success. Furthermore, the representative will build loyalty and trust with customers, creating long-term customer relationships and improving the overall perception of the company's brand.

Empathy is the ability to understand another person's feelings and circumstances. It's a valuable skill that representatives can use when dealing with customers. When a customer has an issue, showing empathy can help to build trust, reduce frustration, and provide a positive customer experience.

In this part, we will discuss what empathy is, why it's important to empathize with customers, and how to effectively exhibit it.

What is Empathy?

Empathy is the ability to put oneself in another person's shoes, to see things from their perspective and understand their emotions. Empathy is different from sympathy because sympathy acknowledges another person's feelings without necessarily understanding them.

Why is it Important to Empathize with Customers?

Empathizing with customers is essential because it shows that representatives understand their issues and want to help. Here are several reasons why empathy is important:

1. **Builds trust** - Demonstrating empathy shows the customer that the representative cares about their issue, which can build trust and rapport.

2. **Provides clarity** - When empathizing, representatives can clarify any misunderstandings, and help customers to articulate their issues better.

3. **Reduces anxiety** - Empathy helps to reduce customer frustration and anxiety, as it can create a more relaxed customer.

4. **Boosts customer satisfaction** - By providing clarity, reducing anxiety and building trust, empathizing can ultimately increase customer satisfaction with the interaction.

How to Effectively Exhibit Empathy

Empathy can be shown in several ways, including:

1. **Active Listening** - The first step in exhibiting empathy is to listen actively to what the customer is saying. Listening actively involves not only hearing what the customer is saying but also paying attention to nonverbal cues, such as tone of voice and body language.

2. **Acknowledging the Customer's Feelings** - It's important to validate the customer's feelings, to show them that their issue is understood, and it matters.

3. **Practical Solutions** - Coming up with practical solutions exhibits that the representative understands the customer's issue and is trying to help solve it.

4. **Following-up** - Following up with the customer ensures that they feel valued and that the representative cares about resolving their issue even after the interaction.

Conclusion

Empathy is a valuable skill for representatives when dealing with customers. By listening actively, acknowledging customers' feelings, providing practical solutions, and following up on issues, representatives can demonstrate empathy and provide a positive customer experience. Empathy shows that the representative understands the customer's issue and wants to help solve it. By practicing empathy, representatives can build trust and rapport, ultimately leading to higher customer satisfaction, and positive customer interactions in the long term.

Dealing with difficult customers can be a high-stress situation for representatives. Work-related stress can lead to burnout, fatigue, and frustration, which in turn can affect the quality of customer interactions. It's vital for representatives to take breaks between customer interactions to maintain optimal levels of productivity and ensure that interactions remain professional and positive.

In this article, we will discuss why taking a break is important when dealing with customers and how it can benefit representatives.

Why Taking a Break is Important

Taking short breaks is essential for representatives when dealing with difficult customers because:

1. **Improves Mental Alertness** - Taking a break increases mental alertness, which can help representatives remain focused on the next interaction.

2. **Reduces Stress** - It's important to break between interactions to reduce stress, as it can help representatives to deal with challenging customers with a clear mind.

3. **Helps to Maintain Professionalism** - By taking a break, representatives can avoid being affected by previous interactions, ensuring that they communicate professionally in future interactions

4. **Helps to Keep Positive Attitude** - Breaks help to maintain a positive attitude, even after dealing with difficult customers, which is critical when dealing with future interactions.

How Taking a Break Can Benefit Representatives

Taking breaks can benefit representatives in several ways:

1. **Reduces Burnout** - Breaks reduce the likelihood of burnout, which happens when a representative feels too much stress and negative emotions at work.

2. **Improves Job Satisfaction** - Taking breaks can increase job satisfaction, as representatives can take time to re-energize and refresh themselves mentally before the next interaction.

3. **Increases Productivity** - By taking a break, representatives can boost productivity by enabling them to focus better on providing efficient and effective customer service.

4. **Enhances Critical Thinking** - By providing downtime, breaks can enable representatives to evaluate customer service interactions, identify and address any gaps, and enhance their critical thinking skills.

Conclusion

Taking a break is essential when dealing with difficult customers. The breaks can help representatives to maintain mental alertness, reduce stress, maintain professionalism, and keep a positive attitude. By taking breaks, representatives reduce the likelihood of burnout, increase job satisfaction, boost productivity, and enhance critical thinking. It's important for representatives to understand the benefits of breaks, and employers to promote the importance of downtime and breaks to enable the representatives to provide the best customer service that ensures optimal productivity and overall work satisfaction.

Setting expectations is a crucial aspect of providing excellent customer service. Customers want to know what to expect when dealing with a company, both in terms of the service they will receive and the outcomes of their interactions. Setting expectations up front can help to manage customer expectations, reduce misunderstandings, and provide a more positive customer experience.

In this article, we will discuss why it's important to set expectations when dealing with customers and how to do it effectively.

Why Setting Expectations is Important

Setting expectations when dealing with customers is essential because:

1. **Helps build trust** - Being transparent about what customers can expect creates trust and helps to build rapport.

2. **Aids in better decision making -** When customers understand outcomes and next steps, they can make informed decisions and feel more confident in their interactions with representatives.

3. **Increases Customer Satisfaction** - By providing a clear understanding of what to expect, customers know what they're getting themselves into, and thus, are more satisfied with the initial experience and interaction.

4. **Reduces uncertainty** - Setting expectations can reduce customer uncertainty and stress, enabling them to communicate more efficiently and seamlessly.

How to Set Expectations Effectively

1. **Be Transparent** - Representatives should be transparent when communicating with customers. Providing complete and honest answers helps to set clear expectations.

2. **Listen to Customers** - Listen to customer inquiries, and if they have concerns or questions, address them to the best of your ability. It will show that you understand their concerns and are willing to address them.

3. **Provide Clear Communication** - Communication is key when dealing with customers. Use clear language and avoid technical jargon that customers may not understand. Make sure that the customer understands the information provided.

4. **Follow Through** - Once expectations have been set, follow through on what has been promised. If the promise is not met, take responsibility, offer options, and put the necessary actions in place to rectify the issue.

5. **Manage Expectations for Challenging Situations** - For challenging situations, such as resolving complaints, representatives may need to set expectations for a longer resolution timeframe, but they should also be transparent in explaining the steps they are taking to resolve the issue.

Conclusion

Setting expectations is a critical aspect of providing excellent customer service. It helps to build trust, reduce uncertainty, and increase customer satisfaction. Representatives can set expectations effectively by being transparent, listening to customers, providing clear communication, following through with commitments, and managing expectations for challenging situations. By setting the right expectations, representatives can manage customer satisfaction, avoid misunderstandings, and provide a more positive interaction, resulting in customer loyalty and long-term relationships.

Part 3 - Communicate effectively

Effective communication is essential for providing great customer service. In a customer service environment, customer satisfaction can very much depend on how effectively you can communicate with them. In this article, we will discuss some tips on how you can improve communication skills to provide excellent customer service.

1. Active Listening

Listening actively, which simply means hearing someone out, is crucial in a customer service role. Listen to your customer's concerns and respond accordingly. Most of your customers just want someone to listen to their problems and help them find a solution.

2. Focus on Positive Language

Instead of saying, "I don't know," try to phrase it positively by saying, "Let me find out for you." Positive language helps to build trust and rapport with your customers and builds confidence in them with you.

3. Be Empathetic & Remain Calm

Put yourself in your customer's shoes and try to understand their perspective. Empathizing with your customers' concerns will make them feel heard and valued, leading to higher customer loyalty. Also, remain calm throughout the conversation, even if a customer is being difficult, and seek to understand the customer.

4. Use Clear and Concise Language

Avoid using technical jargon that your customer might not understand. Use clear and concise language when explaining products or services, and take the time to clarify any questions or concerns a customer might have.

5. Use Positive Body Language

Through video call, it is good to use a positive body language. Maintain eye contact with the customer and smile. If you are interacting over the phone, smile widely as it changes the tone of your voice and make the customer feel good.

Effective communication is a significant contributor to successful customer service. By actively listening to customers, using positive language, being empathetic, using clear & concise language, and using positive body language, you can provide a better overall customer experience. Remember, your ultimate goal is to build strong and lasting relationships with your clients, and excellent communication is fundamental to achieving this success.

Use Positive Language.

Positive language plays a vital role in customer service. It can build trust, resolve conflicts, and create a positive experience for customers. The right choice of words can make the difference between a satisfied customer and an unhappy one. In this article, we will explore the importance of using positive language when talking to customers and offer tips on how to incorporate this into your customer service interactions.

Why is Positive Language Important?

Positive language is an important aspect of communication. It can help de-escalate tense situations, promote understanding, and make customers feel valued. Using positive words and phrases can also make customers feel more confident in your ability to help them, creating a positive association with your brand.

Negative language, on the other hand, can make customers feel disrespected and unappreciated. It can lead to misunderstandings, miscommunications, and even customer churn (customers taking their business elsewhere).

How to Use Positive Language in Customer Service

1. Use Yes Instead of No

Instead of telling customers what you can't do, focus on what you can do. For instance, instead of saying "No, we can't give you a refund," say "Yes, we can offer you a store credit." This makes your customers feel like you are willing to take care of them rather than shutting them down.

2. Use Phrases like "I'll make sure" and "We'll take care of it."

Using phrases such as "I'll make sure" and "We'll take care of it" demonstrates a proactive approach and shows that you are accountable for solutions to customer issues.

3. Focus on solutions.

One of the significant hallmarks of excellent customer service is providing solutions to customers' problems. When communicating with customers, avoid focusing on the issues and instead offer solutions. Use positive language to suggest a course of action.

4. Thank the Customers.

Expressing appreciation to customers is just as essential as addressing their issues. At the end of every interaction, thank the customer for choosing your company and continuing to do business with you.

5. Use Empathy

Being empathetic to customers' needs is also essential when communicating with them. Use positive phrases like "I understand your frustration," or "I see how this is affecting you" to show customers that you care and are on their side.

Conclusion

Positive language is an essential component of great customer service. By using positive words and phrases you can make customers feel valued, respected, and understood, even in the most challenging situations. Incorporating these tips into your customer service interactions will help create a positive experience for customers, which can lead to increased loyalty and revenue for your business. Always remember that in customer service, every word matters, so choose them thoughtfully.

Clear and concise communication is an essential aspect of exceptional customer service. Proper use of language in conversations can enhance understanding and ensure that customers leave conversational settings satisfied. Effective communication between customers and customer service agents can make the customer service process smoother and more efficient. In this article, we will explore the importance of clear and concise language and offer tips on how to incorporate it into customer service interactions.

Why is Clear and Concise Language Important?

Clear and concise language is essential in a customer service environment because it helps to improve communication and ensures that customers understand what they need to know. Using straightforward language enables the customer service representative to communicate the necessary information accurately, making the customer's problem-solving process much easier. The use of complex technical jargon, on the other hand, is likely to cause confusion and frustration to the customers.

How to Use Clear and Concise Language in Customer Service

1. Avoid Jargon.

Many industries develop their language, and because of its complexity, it can become challenging for customers to understand what representatives aim to communicate. Avoiding jargon and other technical terms that may be too technical for the customer is essential. Instead, use simple and clear language to explain what may be technical.

2. Use Examples.

Incorporating examples can help customers understand concepts that may be challenging to comprehend. It creates a clear visual representation of technical issues that may be challenging to explain.

3. Use Short Sentences.

Short sentences make it easier for customers to understand the message being communicated. Using brief sentences makes it possible for the customer to follow the conversation easily and reduces the chance of confusion.

4. Confirm Customer Understands.

It's crucial to ensure that the customer has comprehended all the information communicated. Requesting the customer to clarify anything that may require further understanding exhibits transparency and builds rapport.

5. Avoid Technical Language.

Although technical language can be necessary in the customer service field, it's essential to use technical language only when it's required. Generally, avoiding technical language and using plain language is likely to communicate more effectively with customers.

Conclusion

In conclusion, clear and concise language is a crucial aspect of customer service. By communicating in clear and straightforward language, customer service representatives make it easier for customers to understand and benefit from the services on offer. Remember that customers are relying on your expertise to resolve their issues, so supplanting any technical language with everyday language and checking that the customers understand is key to effective communication. By using the above tips in your customer service interactions, you will create a positive experience for customers, which can lead to customer loyalty and a better reputation for your business.

Part 4 – Maintain a positive attitude

A positive attitude can be the perfect antidote to diffusing a challenging customer service situation. A customer service agent's tone and attitude can significantly influence the outcome of a customer interaction. Maintaining a positive attitude is essential when dealing with customers because it promotes a sense of trust, empathy, and understanding, making the customer feel valued and appreciated. Below are some tips on the importance of a positive attitude in customer service.

1. Empathy

Empathy is the ability to understand and share the feelings of others. Practicing empathy when dealing with customers can help build a positive rapport. Having empathy allows customer service agents to see things from the customer's perspective, which is essential in finding solutions to customer complaints.

2. Active Listening

Active listening is an integral part of effective communication. Customers want to feel heard and understood. Active listening involves paying close attention to what the customer is saying, understanding their needs, and responding appropriately. A positive attitude enhances the active listening process.

3. Stay Positive, Even When It's Challenging

Maintaining a positive attitude, even in challenging situations, can help to diffuse the situation, rather than escalating it. Focus on positive language and offer solutions to customer complaints. Acknowledge the customer's concerns and communicate that you want to help them arrive at a solution.

4. Show Appreciation

Customers want to feel valued and appreciated. Showing appreciation to the customer by thanking them for their business or acknowledging their patience and understanding can go a long way in building a positive rapport.

5. Take Ownership of the Issue

A proactive approach to customer service involves taking ownership of issues and resolving them promptly. A positive attitude instills confidence in the customer, knowing that the agent is actively working to find a solution to their concerns.

Conclusion

Maintaining a positive attitude during customer interactions is essential in providing excellent customer service. A positive attitude fosters a sense of trust and understanding, which can lead to a positive outcome. By following the tips outlined above, customer service agents can build a strong rapport with the customer, while resolving complaints and building brand loyalty. Remember, positivity breeds positivity, so bring positive energy to every customer interaction.

Working in customer service can be challenging, and at times, it can be difficult to maintain a positive attitude. Customers can be demanding, angry, and challenging, making it easy to get discouraged or frustrated. However, staying positive, even in challenging situations, is essential for delivering excellent customer service. In this article, we will explore the importance of staying positive and offer tips on how to maintain a positive attitude in a customer service environment.

Why is staying positive important?

Staying positive in a customer service environment is essential because it promotes better customer interactions. When a customer service agent is positive, it can help to defuse difficult situations and create a sense of trust with the customer. A positive attitude makes it easier to solve problems and find solutions, leading to more satisfied customers. Additionally, a positive attitude can help to reduce stress, increase productivity and create a more pleasant work environment.

Tips for staying positive in a customer service environment

1. Identify and acknowledge your emotions

It's essential to take a moment to identify and acknowledge your emotions, especially when it's a negative one. Acknowledge how you feel, and determine why you feel that way. Is it the customer's attitude or behavior? By identifying the cause of the negative emotion, you can find a solution to manage it.

2. Practice deep breathing

Deep breathing can help alleviate stress and anxiety, which can help to keep a positive attitude. Deep breathing involves inhaling slowly through your nose and exhaling through your mouth. Take long breaths while doing this, and focus on your breath.

3. Look for the positive in every situation

Focus on finding the positive in every situation. For example, if a customer is angry or frustrated, see it as an opportunity to turn the situation around and provide excellent customer service. By focusing on the positive, it can help to maintain a positive perspective.

4. Empathize with the customer

Empathizing with the customer can help to create a sense of understanding and trust. When you put yourself in the customer's shoes, it helps you to approach the situation with an open mind, which can often lead to a positive outcome.

5. Take a break

If you're feeling overwhelmed or stressed, step away from the situation and take a break. Take a walk or engage in another activity that you enjoy doing to help relieve stress.

Conclusion

Maintaining a positive attitude is essential when working in customer service. It can help to create a better experience for customers while reducing stress and frustration for customer service agents. By identifying and acknowledging your emotions, focusing on the positive, empathizing with the customer and taking time to take care of yourself, you can maintain a positive attitude, even in challenging situations. Remember, staying positive takes practice, so be patient with yourself as you develop a positive outlook.

In any customer service environment, one of the most important things to keep in mind is to prioritize showing appreciation to your customers. Fostering a sense of appreciation can go a long way in building loyalty, encouraging repeat business, and ensuring that your customers walk away with a positive experience. There are several ways to show appreciation in a customer service environment, and in this article, we'll explore some of the most effective methods.

1. Thank Your Customer

The simplest yet most effective way to show appreciation towards a customer is to thank them for their patronage. A simple "thank you" can go a long way in making a customer feel valued, especially after a long transaction. Additionally, thanking a customer lets them know that you appreciate their business and their time.

2. Start With a Positive Tone

The way you greet your customers plays a significant role in setting the tone of the interaction. Starting with a positive tone that's warm and welcoming can signal to the customer that they are a valued part of your business. Use friendly language and be approachable from the outset.

3. Personalize Your Interaction

There's nothing quite as gratifying as receiving personalized service. Use the customer's name and reference previous interactions with them to create a more personal experience. This signals that you're interested in their experience with you and have been paying attention to their needs.

4. Show Empathy

Empathy is one of the most critical components of customer service. Customers want to feel heard and understood, and displaying empathy can reassure them that their concerns are valid. Acknowledge their feelings and respond with sensitivity to their concerns.

5. **Offer post-transaction follow-up**

Following up can be an essential part of the appreciation process. Once a transaction is complete, a follow-up call, email, or text message can show additional appreciation. This can be a simple message asking if there is anything else you can do for them, ensuring that they are satisfied with the transaction.

6. **Express Gratitude with small gestures**

Small gestures can have a big impact on how a customer feels about their interaction with you. Providing small tokens of appreciation can send the message that you value their business, such as a personalized note or a small gift.

In conclusion, showing appreciation to customers is essential in a customer service environment. Providing personalized service, displaying empathy, using positive language, and following up after the transaction can foster a sense of appreciation and loyalty. By focusing on your customers and their needs, you can create an environment that values their patronage and encourages them to return for more business.

Taking ownership of the issue is a crucial aspect of delivering excellent customer service that leads to customer loyalty and satisfaction. In a customer service environment, taking ownership means not only taking responsibility for the problem but also working to ensure that it is resolved quickly and effectively. This article will explore the importance of taking ownership of the issue and provide tips on how to do so effectively.

Why is taking ownership of the issue important?

One of the main reasons taking ownership of the issue in customer service is essential is that it shows that you value your customers and are willing to go the extra mile to address their concerns. Customers appreciate feeling that they are in good hands, and taking ownership of the issue can help create that feeling. Additionally, it can help to increase trust between you and the customer, which is crucial in building customer loyalty.

Tips for taking ownership of the issue

1. **Listen actively**

When a customer comes to you with an issue, it's important to listen actively, understand their concern, and show empathy. When a customer feels heard, they are more likely to feel valued and to trust that you are equipped to address their problem.

2. **Take responsibility**

Once you have listened to the customer's concern, it's important to take responsibility for the issue. Acknowledge that there's a problem, and take ownership of the situation, reassuring the customer that their issue is your priority. Even if the issue wasn't caused by your company, taking responsibility shows to the customer that you are committed to finding the solution.

3. **Offer a solution**

After taking ownership of the issue, offer actionable solutions. Clearly communicate, do not oversell and provide them with realistic timelines so they know exactly what to expect. Ensure that the solution you come up with addresses the root of the problem and not just a temporary fix.

4. Stay accountable

After coming up with a solution, make sure to take ownership of the resolution process as well. Communicate how you plan to address the issue and take accountability for ensuring it's resolved in a timely manner. Making promises to customers and forgetting can be detrimental to your credibility and how your customer perceives your customer service.

5. Follow up

Following up is key when it comes to taking ownership of the issue. Once you have provided a solution, make sure to check back in with the customer to ensure that the issue is resolved and they are satisfied. This helps in building relationship and trust with the customer.

Conclusion

Taking ownership of the issue is a critical component of delivering excellent customer service in any industry. By actively listening to customers, taking responsibility for the problem, offering a solution, staying accountable, and following up, you can show your customers that you care about their concerns and appreciate their business. Taken together, these steps can make the difference for a business to maintain its customer base and increase loyalty. By implementing these customer service principles and taking ownership of customer issues, businesses can turn potential failures into opportunities for growth and lasting customer satisfaction.

Part 5 – Attention To Detail

Attention to detail is crucial when dealing with customers. It enables customer service representatives to identify problems, anticipate customers' needs, and provide high-quality services that meet or exceed customers' expectations. Here are some tips for attention to detail when dealing with customers.

1. Active listening

Active listening is a crucial skill for paying attention to detail when dealing with customers. It involves paying close attention to clients, clarifying their needs, and interpreting their feedback correctly. An attentive listener can pick up on subtle nuances in conversation and address them accordingly. Listening also involves providing feedback to convey the message that you've heard what the customer has to say accurately.

2. Ask questions

Asking questions can help customer service representatives to gather critical information from customers. Quality questions can help to uncover problems, catch errors, and align the customer's desires with the available solutions. By specifically and directly asking questions, a customer service representative can have a detailed understanding of the issue.

3. Evaluate non-verbal cues

Nonverbal communication can also provide valuable clues to a customer's needs or emotions. Customer service representatives should lean into body language, tone of voice, or facial expressions. By evaluating non-verbal cues, customer service representatives can understand better how the customer feels, providing information on how to respond appropriately.

4. Doing a "check and correct" routine

By following a "check and correct" routine, customers will receive consistent responses using a comprehensive approach. This means regularly auditing written or verbal scripts to ensure they are up to date, accurate and providing a satisfactory resolution to the issues being addressed.

5. Multitasking ability

During customer interactions, a service representative must be able to process a large amount of information while efficiently multitasking to address the customer's concerns. The ability to prioritize and multitask effectively helps in addressing individual needs while providing great service to other callers.

6. Practice empathy

Empathy has a significant role in achieving an excellent level of attention to detail. By placing oneself in the customer's position when addressing each concern, a representative can provide quality service that can meet their clients' distinct needs.

In conclusion, attention to detail when dealing with customers is critical to successful service delivery. Customer service representatives need to be active listeners, ask the right questions, evaluate nonverbal cues, maintain accuracy through "check and correct," multitasking ability, and practice empathy when interacting with customers. With these tips, businesses can provide better customer service that fosters loyalty, retention, and trustworthiness.

In a customer service environment, asking questions is a vital component of providing excellent service to clients. The questions asked can help determine the root cause of a problem, identify the customer's needs, and gather crucial information to navigate the situation. Additionally, asking questions can demonstrate to the customer that they are important and that their concerns are being taken seriously. In this article, we explore the importance of asking questions in a customer service environment and provide tips on how to ask the right questions effectively.

Identifying the customer's needs

Asking questions is essential in identifying a customer's needs. Not all customers will clearly articulate their needs, and it is the responsibility of the service representative to probe and understand the customer's problem better. By asking questions, service representatives can identify the priority issues and address them. This process creates a collaborative effort between the customer and the service representative and allows both parties to exchange information and understanding.

Better understanding the root cause of a problem

Many times, customers will come with one concern, but the request is more significant than the issue presented. Active listening and asking questions allow customer service representatives to identify the root cause of a problem. If customer service representatives do not ask the right questions, they risk trying to address only the surface level problem, neglecting the significant issue.

Gathering the necessary information

When dealing with customer issues, gathering the right information is critical to developing a solution. Efficiently gathering a complete picture of the customer's issue can ensure that the appropriate departments or individuals resolve the problem. The right set of questions can help ensure the service representative has all the necessary information to address the problem effectively.

Demonstrates Empathy

Asking the right question shows customers that the service representatives are concerned, empathetic, and willing to help. When service representatives actively ask questions with a genuine intention to understand the customer's needs, they can create a rapport to address the customer's problem.

Tips for asking the right questions

Given that the purpose of asking questions is to create a cooperative effort and identify the customer's problem, below are tips for asking the right questions:

1. Active listening

Active listening is crucial when asking the right questions. By carefully observing and understanding the customer's concerns, service representatives can immerse themselves in the situation and provide fact-based solutions.

2. Be Clear and concise

Service representatives need to ask clear and concise questions to avoid ambiguity or misunderstanding. Ambiguous questions lead to irrelevant or ineffective answers, leading to wasted time and lost opportunities at resolving the customer's issue.

3. Avoid multiple questions in a single statement.

Asking multiple questions risks the customer being confused or unwilling to answer. Instead, it is best to ask a single question at a time to ensure a quick response to requiring minimal explanation.

4. Allow for open-ended questions.

Open-ended questions allow the customer to share relevant information and provide insight into the problem. This feedback can help to gain a better understanding of the context and provide the correct solution.

5. Ask clarifying questions

When customers do not articulate their concerns, it's important to follow up with questions to clarify the issue. Clarifying information will ensure that the service representative provides accurate solutions.

Conclusion

Asking questions in a customer service environment is a vital aspect of solving customer problems. Asking relevant, clear, and concise questions can enable the service representative to understand the customer's needs, identify the root cause of the problem, gather necessary information, shows empathy and provide the best possible solution. Ultimately, when service representatives can ask the right questions in a customer service, it can lead to improved customer satisfaction, repeat business, and customer referrals, all which fuel a growing business.

In any kind of customer service interaction, non-verbal cues can be just as important as the words spoken. Understanding and evaluating non-verbal cues are critical in improving communication, identifying potential problems, and addressing customer needs. Non-verbal communication includes body language, tone of voice, facial expressions, gestures and eye contact. In this article, we explore the importance of evaluating non-verbal cues when dealing with customers, and how it can boost customer satisfaction.

Non-verbal communication can convey emotional states, attitudes, and intentions. For example, the way a customer speaks, their tone of voice, body posture, and facial expressions provide vital clues to their state of mind. This communication presents an opportunity for customer service representatives to identify frustration or satisfaction, and address the customer's needs accordingly. Here are some key reasons evaluating non-verbal cues in a customer service environment is crucial:

Understanding emotions

One of the primary reasons for evaluating non-verbal cues is for the service representative to understand the customer's emotions. Emotions hidden in tone, gestures or facial expressions can mean unspoken concerns or frustrations. Identifying these emotions before proceeding with a conversation allows the service representative to adjust their approach and answer to the customer's emotional state. The service representative may then effectively understand the customer's problem, acknowledge their emotions, and resolve the issue in the best possible attitude.

Establishing trust

Successful customer service is dependent on establishing trust with the customer. When the customer perceives that the service representative is actively listening and aware of their non-verbal communications, it builds trust with the company. Trust is the foundation of the ongoing relationship with the customer since they will feel they can rely on the company for future needs.

Resolving conflict

Conflict resolution is another area that evaluating non-verbal cues can be advantageous. By understanding non-verbal signals like tense body language, a customer representative identifies the customer's frustrations and resolve the issue. Alternatively, when customer representatives respond in a threatening or confrontational way, they risk escalating the situation. Thus, evaluations of a customer's non-verbal cues are critical in identifying conflict resolution openings.

Offering personalized solutions.

Evaluating non-verbal cues are also important since it can help identify what a customer specifically needs at the moment. By understanding their emotions, facial expressions, and tone of voice, customer service representatives receive insight into a customer's situation, allowing for personalized responses. Personalized solutions increase customer satisfaction, minimize the need for follow-up communication and make the customer feel valued.

Tips for Evaluating Non-Verbal Cues

Effective evaluation of non-verbal communication requires specific skills. Here are a few tips to keep in mind:

Listen actively to the tone of the customer's voice, it can indicate frustration or satisfaction.

Look for involuntary emotions that give insight into the customer's feelings.

Gestures and postures provide important context to what words conceal, pay attention to them during the conversation.

Stay engaged and present, avoid being preoccupied, or distracted.

Consciously show interest through facial expressions and body language.

Conclusion

In a customer service environment, evaluating non-verbal cues can positively impact the interaction with customers. Through keen observation, good listening skills, and astute insight, customer service representatives can identify unspoken needs or frustrations and work towards addressing them. With the right approach, evaluating non-verbal cues will help service representatives offer personalized solutions, establish trust, and resolve conflicts effectively. These qualities are critical to delivering excellent customer service resulting in customer satisfaction and loyalty.

In a customer service environment, it is essential to establish and maintain quality control practices, ensuring that service consistently meets the highest standards. One such practice is a "check and correct" routine. Check and correct identifies opportunities for improvement, monitors quality benchmarks, and helps ensure the customer's expectations are met. In this article, we explore how to do a check and correct routine in customer service, its benefits, and best practices to follow for quality assurance.

What is a Check and Correct Routine?

A check and correct routine is a quality control practice that involves checking the work carried out by the customer service representative and correcting it if necessary. A representative can check and balance their work by comparing it to recognized quality benchmarks, analyzing customer feedback and reviewing performance indicators. Importantly, a check and correct routine seeks to identify opportunities for improvement with the end goal of improving customer satisfaction.

Benefits of a Check and Correct Routine

Implementing a check and correct routine in customer services has numerous advantages, including:

Improved customer experience:
A check and correct routine helps guarantee that customer issues are resolved correctly on the first attempt and meet the expectations of the customer. Improving the overall customer experience helps to build satisfaction and customer loyalty.

Increased Efficiency:
Check and correct helps identify areas that need improvement, such as procedures or processes that may vary between agents. By addressing these areas and establishing best practices, customers can be assisted in a more efficient manner.

Clear Standards:

A check and correct routine, provides a baseline or clear standard of performance, helps ensure consistency of service across the customer service channels.

Quality control:
Check and correct routine helps maintain a high standard of quality, ensuring that every customer service representative delivers consistent service and meets the company's defined quality standards.

Best Practices for Conducting Check and Correct

To ensure a successful check and correct routine, adhere to best practices for carrying out this practice.

Set Clear Standards:
Design and establish key performance Indicators(KPI) for quick identification of potential areas of improvement, compare to best-practice benchmarks and tailor continuous improvement programs in response.

Be Proactive:
Identify potential problems before they arise by reviewing traditional data points such as customer complaints or customer satisfaction surveys.

Adopt a system-based approach:
Utilize a centralized software or database to record customer interactions, follow-ups, and evaluations. Centralization ensures that customer service representatives can access pertinent information in real-time, improving service results.

Implement Peer Review:
Peer review, involving customer service agents also provides suggestions for improvement, and ensures that customer service representatives adhere to protocols and standards.

Provide Feedback and reinforcement:
Provide positive reinforcement to those who demonstrate solid customer service skills, and offer constructive feedback to those who require improvement.

Ensure Regular Review:
Make sure to routinely schedule reviews, this process will stimulate a culture of continuous improvement that always works towards providing the best possible customer experience.

Here are some examples of how a check and correct routine may be used in customer service:

1. **Recording and reviewing calls:** Customer service representatives may record customer calls to evaluate their performance. By listening to their own calls, agents can assess their tone, communication skills, and whether they were able to resolve customer concerns properly. Supervisors may also listen to calls to offer feedback and identify performance areas that require improvement.

2. **Reviewing customer feedback:** Customer feedback is an essential input to help service providers understand how their products and services are perceived. Companies can collect feedback through surveys via email, social media, or in-person interactions. Aggregated insights from customer feedback enable the company to make informed decisions about product and service improvements based on the identified trends or concerns.

3. **Internal Quality Monitoring:** This involves monitoring customer interactions to ensure that a service representative is adhering to defined protocols and procedures. It enables the identification of areas in which additional training and skill development may be needed.

4. **Benchmarking against industry standards:** A company may analyze metrics from peer groups or competitors to assess how they are performing against industry standards for service delivery. The analysis can include objective measures such as time taken to resolve an issue, or it may be subjective, such as customer feedback ratings.

5. **Using software assists:** Software assists such as chatbots allow the company to monitor conversations across channels. Monitoring the chatbots enables the company to develop frequently-asked-questions-style prompts, analyze chat history to improve responses, facilitate staff responsibility and trace the tone and characteristic of response in a live interaction.

By utilizing a range of check and correct routines, companies can identify areas of improvement, maintain quality standards, and ensure customer satisfaction. Determining how to implement them requires the company to look within and analyze the interactions, practices, and procedures they currently use. Once implemented with some repeated tests, a company can ensure that company expectations for service delivery are institutionalized while guaranteeing customer satisfaction.

Conclusion:

A check and correct method is an essential and effective process that can be implemented in customer services to identify areas of improvement, maintain quality standards, and ensure customer satisfaction. When correctly conducted, a check and correct process ensures that the right service is provided a just the right time, offering customers hghly-reliable, timely and high-quality solutions. Adopting a check and correct routine ensures that customer service representatives are equipped with the tools they require to provide exceptional customer service, promote customer satisfaction and build brand loyalty.

Multitasking in customer service is an essential skill that allows service providers to handle multiple tasks at once. Efficient multitasking allows customer service representatives to stay organized, manage their time effectively, and handle customer queries and concerns simultaneously. In this article, we will explore the importance of multitasking in customer service and provide some tips to improve your multitasking abilities.

Importance of Multitasking in Customer Service

In customer service, multitasking is critical as service providers must address multiple customer concerns simultaneously, maintain the highest levels of customer satisfaction, and ensure that all service requests are resolved promptly. Efficient multitasking helps customer service representatives to handle multiple tasks and address customer needs effectively while maintaining a high level of productivity.

In customer service, multitasking helps to:

> 1. **Improve Response Times:** Multitasking allows representatives to complete multiple customer requests simultaneously, reducing response times and ensuring that customers do not experience unnecessary delays.
>
> 2. **Enhance Efficiency**: By having the ability to handle multiple customer requests at once, customer service representatives can increase their productivity, allowing them to handle more customers in a shorter amount of time, improving efficiency.
>
> 3. **Provide Flexibility**: Multitasking allows customer service representatives to be more adaptable and to shift their priorities quickly if a critical customer issue arises.

Tips for Multitasking in Customer Service

While multitasking can be highly beneficial for customer service, it requires a certain skill set and a focused approach to succeed. Here are some tips to help you successfully multitask and provide excellent customer service:

1. **Prioritize:** Assign priorities to the tasks you need to complete during a workday to allow for efficient handling of critical tasks first. Using a task management tool can be highly beneficial in monitoring tasks, and what needs to be done next.

2. **Focus:** Avoid distractions and stay focused on the tasks at hand. Eliminating distractions such as social media and mobile notifications allows for a more focused approach.

3. **Use Time Management Techniques:** Time management techniques like Pomodoro can help manage time and improve focus skills. Utilizing techniques such as Pomodoro, it comprises breaks in between focused work sessions of 25 minutes and provides a more managed approach through which employees can work more effectively.

4. **Follow Standard Protocols:** Follow the processes and rules laid down by the company to ensure that you address customer issues effectively while staying focused on multiple tasks.

5. **Be Empathetic:** While multitasking, ensure to be empathetic and connect with customers effectively. It is essential to keep the customer experience in focus while avoiding any negative effect of multitasking on the customer experience.

Conclusion:

In customer service, multitasking is an essential skill that enables customer service representatives to handle multiple queries, complaints, and support requests simultaneously. Efficient multitasking improves response times, enhances efficiency, and provides flexibility for customer service representatives to manage multiple tasks effectively. Effective multitasking in customer service relies on strong prioritization, focus, time management, adherence to procedures or protocols, empathy, and ensuring that the customer's experience is not compromised. With the right approach and practice, multitasking can drive improved customer service and satisfaction, ultimately boosting your company's reputation and bottom line.

Part 6 – Conflict Resolution

Conflict resolution in customer service is an essential skill that can make or break customer relationships. When customers experience a problem, they often seek help from customer service representatives to find a solution. However, sometimes conflicts can arise between customers and customer service representatives that can be challenging to resolve. In this article, we will discuss effective conflict resolution tips to follow in customer service.

1. **Listen actively:** Listening actively to understand the root cause of the customer's complaint is the first step to conflict resolution. Ensure that you give your undivided attention to the customer and encourage them to express themselves freely. Avoid interrupting them, and try to clarify any misunderstandings to get a clear picture of their problem.

2. **Empathize with the customer**: Empathizing is a key skill in customer service that enables the service provider to connect with the customer emotionally. When handling conflicts, use language that demonstrates your understanding of the problem, and acknowledge how the customer feels. This helps to build trust and strengthens the customer's confidence in your ability to resolve the situation.

3. **Find common ground:** Finding common ground with the customer can help to resolve potential conflicts. Try to identify an area of agreement or shared goal that you and the customer can work towards, which can help build a collaborative environment that results in a satisfactory solution.

4. **Provide options and alternatives:** If the customer's issue is not easily resolvable, provide options or suggest alternatives that could address the customer's issue. Advise the customer that you are committed to finding a solution that meets their needs.

5. **Offer a sincere apology:** If the customer is upset or annoyed, offering a sincere apology can be an effective way to resolve the conflict. Even if the issue was not your fault, apologizing for the inconvenience can demonstrate that you care about the customer's experience and want to make things right.

6. **Follow through:** Once a resolution has been reached, follow

through on any commitments made to the customer. Ensure that the chosen solution is implemented and that the customer is satisfied with the result. Follow-up with your customer after the interaction to ensure they feel that their issue was fully resolved.

Conclusion:

Effective conflict resolution is an essential skill for customer service representatives. Listening actively, empathizing with the customer, finding common ground, providing options and alternatives, offering sincere apologies, and following through are all important steps in conflict resolution. By using these techniques, customer service representatives can create a positive customer experience and build strong customer relationships, even in the face of conflict.

When customers experience a problem, they often seek help from customer service representatives to find a solution. However, sometimes conflicts can arise between customers and customer service representatives that can be difficult to resolve. One effective way to resolve conflicts is to find common ground. In this article, we will discuss what is meant by common ground and how to find common ground during conflict resolution in customer services.

What is Common Ground?

Common ground refers to shared beliefs, values, and goals that people can cultivate to develop a mutual understanding. When two parties have found common ground, they can move forward from a shared starting point with a clear understanding of what both parties need or want. In the context of conflict resolution, finding common ground can lead to a resolution that is satisfactory for everyone involved.

How to Find Common Ground During Conflict Resolution in Customer Services?

1. Identify the Issue

The first step in finding common ground is to identify the issue clearly. Ensure that the problem is specific and concise, and avoid making assumptions or generalizations. Confirm that you have a mutual understanding of the issue and agree on what needs to be addressed.

2. Acknowledge Emotions

Acknowledge the customer's emotions and feelings about the problem they are facing. Let them know that you understand their frustration or concern and validate their point of view.

3. Listen Actively

Listening actively to the customer is essential in finding common ground. Remain attentive, and ask open-ended questions to gain a full understanding of the customer's perspective. This approach can help to establish trust and show the customer that you are committed to finding a solution.

4. Focus on Solutions

When trying to find common ground, avoid focusing on who is right or wrong. Instead, concentrate on finding solutions that meet the needs of both parties. Seek to understand the customer's expectations and offer options that could address the issue.

5. Brainstorm Options

Invite the customer to brainstorm options with you. Encourage them to think creatively and suggest solutions that may have never been considered before. This approach helps to build a collaborative environment in which both parties work together actively to find a resolution.

6. Evaluate Solutions Together

Once a range of possible solutions has been identified, it's important to evaluate the options together. Consider both the positive and negative aspects of each proposed solution to develop a comprehensive list of pros and cons.

7. Choose a Solution That Works for Both Parties

After evaluating the solutions, select the option that meets the needs of both the customer and the company. Ensure that the solution is feasible and fits within company policies and procedures.

Conclusion

In summary, finding common ground during conflict resolution can be an effective way to find satisfactory solutions for both customers and companies in customer services. By identifying the issue, acknowledging emotions, listening actively, focusing on solutions, brainstorming options, evaluating solutions together, and choosing a mutually beneficial solution, customer service representatives can build strong relationships and create positive experiences for customers. When both parties can find common ground and work together, the result is a successful resolution to the conflict.

Customer service representatives often find themselves in situations where they have to resolve conflicts with unhappy or dissatisfied customers. Resolving conflicts requires an aptitude for excellent communication skills and the ability to provide satisfactory solutions that meet the needs of both the customer and the company. In some situations, providing options and alternatives can be an effective strategy in conflict resolution. In this article, we'll explore the importance of providing options and alternatives when dealing with conflict resolutions in customer service.

Why Provide Options and Alternatives?

When a customer is dissatisfied or unhappy, offering only one solution may not always resolve the issue. By providing options and alternatives, you give the customer a sense of control over their situation and provide them with choices. This approach fosters customer rapport and trust, and can result in a more satisfactory resolution.

Options and alternatives also demonstrate the company's commitment to customer satisfaction. By presenting multiple options, you show that you are willing to work with the customer to find a resolution that addresses their issue and meets their needs.

How to Provide Options and Alternatives During Conflict Resolution

1. Listen Actively

When dealing with conflict resolution in customer service, active listening is critical. It's essential to gain a clear understanding of the customer's concerns and needs. By actively listening, you can assess the situation accurately and identify what solutions might be appropriate.

2. Offer a Range of Solutions

When providing options and alternatives, present a range of solutions that reflect the customer's preferences and company policies. Be sure to provide clear explanations for each solution, so that the customer can evaluate the benefits and drawbacks of each option.

3. Explain the Consequences

It's important to explain the consequences of each solution you present to the customer. Discuss how each option could impact the customer and the company. Explain any limitations, costs or benefits of each solution, and be transparent about how each solution could affect the customer's concern.

4. Consider the Long-Term Impacts

When providing options and alternatives, consider the long-term impacts for both the customer and the company. Look for win-win scenarios that offer long-term benefits for the customer and company. Be sure to consider the impact on all stakeholders involved.

5. Confirm the Customer Understands the Options and Alternatives

Before proceeding with the chosen solution, confirm that the customer understands the options and alternatives offered to them, and that they agree with the choice. This ensures that the customer is fully informed and aware of the consequences of their decision.

Conclusion

Providing options and alternatives during conflict resolution in customer service can be an effective strategy in finding a satisfactory solution for both the customer and company. By actively listening, offering a range of solutions, explaining the consequences, considering the long-term impact and confirming the customer's understanding, customer service representatives can resolve conflicts effectively and foster positive customer experiences. By offering options and alternatives, you can provide the customer with a sense of control over their situation, and this often improves their satisfaction with the interaction.

When dealing with customer complaints, a sincere apology can go a long way in resolving an issue and restoring positive customer relations. Apologizing correctly can make a big difference in how a customer perceives the situation and how the situation is resolved. In this article, we will discuss the importance of offering a sincere apology during conflict resolution in customer service and how to apologize sincerely when dealing with customer complaints.

Why is Offering a Sincere Apology Important?

Apologizing during conflict resolution is crucial because it validates the customer's feelings, acknowledges their concerns and shows empathy. A sincere apology demonstrates a company's commitment to resolving grievances and improving their customer service.

Offering a sincere apology can also help to de-escalate a tense or heated situation. Acknowledging a customer's frustration or disappointment can ease tension and help establish trust between the customer and the customer service representative.

How to Apologize Sincerely During Conflict Resolution

1. Use a Personalized Approach

When offering an apology, use a personalized approach that directly addresses the customer's concerns. Speak to customers using their name and mention their specific complaint. This approach demonstrates that you have listened to their concerns and that you understand their situation.

2. Express Empathy

Express empathy when apologizing to customers. This helps the customer feel heard and understood. Acknowledge their frustration, concern or anger and provide an explanation for the situation. An apology accompanied by empathy can go a long way toward resolving the customer's issue.

3. Accept Responsibility

Accept responsibility for any mistakes or shortcomings and apologize genuinely. Be clear about the company's policies and take ownership of any issues that may have arisen. Don't make excuses or shift blame.

4. Offer a Solution

After apologizing, offer a solution to make things right. This may include refunds, exchanges or simply an explanation of how to avoid a similar situation in the future. Offering a solution is a way to move forward from the situation and restore customer confidence in your company.

5. Follow-up with the Customer

Following up with the customer after the apology is equally important. It demonstrates that you are committed to the resolution of the issue, and gives the customer an opportunity to express any concerns or to provide feedback about the solution. This gesture shows that the apology was not just an empty promise, but a genuine effort to support the customer.

Conclusion

In customer service, saying sorry appropriately and accepting responsibility for any mistakes or shortcomings can demonstrate a company's commitment to excellence in customer relations. It takes courage and humility to apologize, but it can help to create positive customer experiences and foster customer loyalty. By using a personalized approach, expressing empathy, accepting responsibility, offering a solution, and following up with the customer, customer service representatives can offer a sincere apology and restore customer trust in the company.

When it comes to conflict resolution in customer service, following through is key to maintaining positive customer relationships. It's not enough to simply resolve a customer's complaint; following up to ensure that the issue has been resolved can provide peace of mind to the customer and help to build trust between the customer and the company. In this article, we'll discuss the importance of following through after conflict resolution in customer service and provide tips on how to follow through effectively.

Why Following Through is Important

Following through after conflict resolution shows your customers that their issue is important to you and that you are committed to providing exceptional customer service. It also demonstrates that you have taken the necessary measures to resolve their issue, a gesture that is highly appreciated by customers. In addition, following through can lead to positive word-of-mouth recommendations from the customer, which can be beneficial for the business.

Tips for Following Through After Conflict Resolution

1. Set Clear Expectations

When resolving a customer's issue, be clear about what actions you will take and the timeframe in which those actions will be taken. Make sure the customer understands what to expect and when they should expect it. This will help to avoid misunderstandings and confusion later on.

2. Follow Up in a Timely Manner

Following up with the customer in a timely manner is crucial. Make sure you contact the customer within the agreed-upon timeframe or as soon as possible. This shows the customer that their time and concern is important to you and that you are committed to resolving their issue quickly.

3. Confirm That the Issue is Resolved

When following up, confirm that the issue has been resolved to the customer's satisfaction. You can do this by asking the customer directly, conducting a satisfaction survey, or checking in with the customer after a few days to ensure that the resolution has been effective.

4. Thank the Customer for Their Feedback

Customers who provide feedback are valuable to the company, as they help to identify areas for improvement. Thank the customer for their feedback and ask for suggestions on how the company can improve its products or services. This gesture shows that you value their opinion and are committed to continuously enhancing the customer experience.

5. Document the Resolution

Document the resolution in the customer's account or file so that other representatives or departments can refer to the resolution if the customer contacts the company again in the future. This step can help to avoid misunderstandings or repeated resolutions for the same issue.

Conclusion

Following through after conflict resolution in customer service helps to maintain positive customer relationships and shows the customer that their issue is important to the company. Setting clear expectations, following up in a timely manner, confirming that the issue has been resolved to the customer's satisfaction, thanking the customer for their feedback, and documenting the resolution are all steps that can help to make the follow-through process effective. By following these tips, companies can build positive customer experiences and foster customer loyalty.

Product knowledge is essential in providing quality customer service. Customers expect representatives to be knowledgeable about the products or services being offered, and to be able to answer any questions they may have. In this article, we will provide tips on how to improve and maintain product knowledge in customer service.

1. Study the Product

One of the best ways to improve product knowledge is to study the product. Take the time to review product literature, user manuals, and other relevant materials that will help to understand how the product works. This will give you a better understanding of the product details, and you will have more knowledge to answer the customer's questions.

2. Regular Training

Companies should invest in regular training to ensure that customer service representatives are up to date with the latest product offerings and changes. Training can be delivered by internal experts or through external training providers. Regular training can help to keep staff knowledgeable and motivated.

3. Use the Product Yourself

The best way to learn about a product is to use it yourself. By using the product, you will experience its features and functionalities firsthand, and you will be better equipped to answer customer questions. This familiarity will also help in providing an authentic and personal review of the product to customers

4. Practice Active Listening

Active listening is key in identifying customer needs and concerns. Listen attentively to customer inquiries and take note of the questions asked frequently. Understanding your customers needs will help you to match the right product solutions to their issues.

5. Collaborate with other Teams

Collaborating with other departments can help customer service representatives to better understand the product and how to address customer concerns. For example, representatives can work with the sales team or technical support team to gain knowledge and insights on the product features and functionalities.

6. Provide Solutions

Customers expect timely, effective solutions when encountering product related issues. Your product knowledge will help you to provide a solution to customer concerns. Offer alternatives and workarounds or escalate to experienced representatives if an issue is too technical to handle.

Conclusion

Product knowledge is key to providing quality customer service. The more knowledgeable a representative is about a product or service, the easier it is to identify customer needs and provide effective solutions. Studying the product, participating in regular training, using the product, practicing active listening, collaborating with other teams, and providing effective solutions are all excellent ways to improve and maintain product knowledge in customer service. By following these tips, customer service representatives can deliver exceptional service and foster customer loyalty.

Part 8 – Effective Time Management

Time management is essential to success in a customer service environment. Representatives must be able to effectively manage their time to handle customer inquiries promptly while maintaining quality service. In this article, we will provide tips on how to manage time effectively in a customer service environment.

1. **Prioritize Tasks**

A key element of time management is to prioritize tasks. Evaluate and organize tasks based on their urgency and importance. For example, if there is a high volume of incoming customer service calls, prioritize answering the phone over checking emails.

2. **Use Time Management Tools**

There are many tools available to help with time management, from physical planners to digital apps. Use these tools to create a schedule and prioritize tasks. Take advantage of scheduling features to block off time slots for specific tasks, such as responding to customer emails or returning phone calls. This will help to ensure time is spent efficiently.

3. **Plan for Emergencies**

Emergencies can happen, so it is important to be prepared. Develop a plan for unexpected situations, such as a high volume of calls, technical issues, or sudden spikes in inquiries. Developing a plan ensures that the customer service team is equipped to handle emergency situations promptly.

4. **Set Realistic Expectations**

Be realistic about the time needed to complete tasks. Set achievable goals and prioritize them effectively. Over-promising and under-delivering will lead to frustration from both the representative and the customer.

5. **Develop Time Management Skills**

Developing good time management habits can be challenging but will help you in the long run. Plan and execute tasks systematically. Take breaks when needed to relieve stress and stay refreshed.

6. Use Automation

Automation can help to streamline processes in a customer service environment. Use automated email responses for common inquiries to reduce the workload. Implement self-service options to allow users to find answers to common questions on a website. Utilizing these features can help to save time and increase efficiency.

Conclusion

Time management is crucial in a customer service environment. Prioritizing tasks, using time management tools, planning for emergencies, setting realistic expectations, developing time management skills, and using automation are all ways to improve time management in customer service. These practices can help to not only improve efficiency but also improve the customer experience by providing prompt and effective service.

Time management is a critical skill in customer service, where representatives must balance a wide variety of tasks while providing excellent service to customers. By prioritizing their workload strategically, customer service representatives can ensure that they get the most important tasks completed first, while minimizing stress and increasing productivity. In this article, we will provide practical tips on how to prioritize tasks for time management in customer service.

1. Identify Urgent and Important Tasks

The first step to effective task prioritization is to determine the most urgent and important tasks. This involves identifying tasks that must be completed immediately to ensure that customers' needs are satisfied. For example, tasks such as responding to high-priority customer inquiries, resolving urgent complaints, and handling escalated issues should be at the top of the priority list.

2. Evaluate the Level of Effort Required

Once urgent tasks have been identified, customer service representatives should evaluate the level of effort needed to complete each task. Some tasks may be quick and easy to complete, while others may require more time and energy. Tasks that are more complex or require significant effort should be prioritized higher, as they may take longer to complete.

3. Consider Customer Impact

The next step in prioritizing tasks is to consider how each task will impact customers. Representatives should focus on tasks that are most critical to customer satisfaction and address customer complaints and requests that are the most pressing. This will help to build trust and confidence with customers and show that their needs are a top priority.

4. Determine Deadlines

When prioritizing tasks, representatives should also be aware of deadlines. Whether it's an internal deadline or a customer-requested due date, it's important to ensure that all tasks are completed on time. Tasks that have a looming deadline or a high level of importance to the customer should be completed promptly to avoid potential delays that could negatively affect the customer experience.

5. Schedule Time for Each Task

After prioritizing tasks, representatives should allocate sufficient time for each task to ensure they are completed effectively. This involves breaking down larger tasks into smaller subtasks and setting specific deadlines for each subtask. Scheduling dedicated time for each task ensures that they get the attention and focus they need to be completed to a high standard.

6. Reassess and Adjust Priorities Continuously

Lastly, customer service representatives should continuously monitor and reassess their priorities. New tasks and demands may emerge throughout the day that require them to shift their focus or re-prioritize their workload. Regularly reassessing priorities and making adjustments ensures that representatives are always focusing on the most important tasks and providing the best possible service to customers.

Conclusion

Effective task prioritization is key to time management in customer service. By identifying urgent and important tasks, evaluating effort and customer impact, determining deadlines, scheduling time for each task, and continuously reassessing priorities, representatives can maximize productivity while providing excellent customer service. Implementing these strategies can help customer service teams to effectively manage their workload and reduce stress, while also increasing customer satisfaction and building trust.

Time management is a crucial skill that customer service representatives need to develop to deliver excellent service to customers. In today's fast-paced business environment, customer service representatives need to be efficient and productive to handle multiple tasks and meet customer needs. Fortunately, various time management tools can help customer service representatives stay organized, manage their time effectively, and improve customer service. In this article, we will discuss some of the best time management tools that customer service representatives can use to improve customer service.

1. To-Do List and Task Managers

To-do lists and task managers are one of the best time management tools that customer service representatives can use to stay organized and prioritize tasks. With the help of these tools, representatives can quickly identify which tasks need to be completed first and track progress towards completing them. Some popular task management tools include Trello, Asana, Todoist, and Microsoft Planner.

2. Calendar Tools

Calendar tools are another crucial time management tool that customer service representatives must utilize. With calendar tools such as Google Calendar, Microsoft Outlook, and Apple Calendar, customer service representatives can schedule their tasks and appointments effectively. Representatives can also set reminders, block off dedicated work hours, and coordinate with their team members' schedules to avoid scheduling conflicts.

3. Time Tracking Software

Time tracking software can help customer service representatives analyze how they allocate their time and determine tasks that consume more time than they should. Time tracking tools like Toggl and Harvest can help representatives monitor how they manage their time and devise strategies that improve their time management skills.

4. Automated Apps

Customer service representatives can automate and streamline their workflow using online tools and applications. Online apps such as Zapier, IFTTT, and Microsoft Flow can help in automating most of the tedious tasks such as social media posting, file transfers, and email reminders. This frees up valuable time for customer service representatives to focus on other important tasks.

5. Browser Extensions

Browser extensions such as StayFocusd, and Pomodoro trackers can help representatives stay focused and avoid distractions during work hours. StayFocusd can block time-wasting sites, Pomodoro trackers help in breaking down long-term tasks to manageable intervals, and both tools can help in improving overall work efficiency.

Conclusion

Effective time management is critical for providing excellent customer service. Customer service representatives can use time management tools to streamline their workflow, stay organized, and manage their time effectively. By using tools such as task managers, calendar tools, time tracking software, automated apps, and browser extensions, customer service representatives can increase productivity, lower stress levels, and provide the best customer service possible. Customer service teams that incorporate these tools into their daily operations can expect to see a significant improvement in customer satisfaction levels.

Effective time management in customer service involves preparing for and managing emergency situations. It's important for customer service representatives to be proactive in planning for emergencies, having a solid plan in place, and being able to respond quickly and efficiently to urgent customer needs. In this article, we'll discuss the importance of planning for emergencies and how customer service representatives can prepare for these situations to ensure the best possible customer experience.

Why Planning for Emergencies is Important

The nature of customer service is inherently unpredictable, and emergencies can happen at any time. These emergencies can include power outages, system failures, natural disasters, communication breakdowns, or individual customer issues that require immediate attention. Being able to handle these emergencies effectively can make the difference between keeping a customer loyal and losing them.

Without proper preparation, these emergencies can take the customer service team off guard, which can lead to chaos and a loss of customer confidence. Poor management of these emergencies can also lead to missed opportunities to resolve issues quickly, which can further frustrate customers and cause reputational harm to the company.

How to Plan for Emergencies in Time Management

1. Identify Potential Emergencies

The first step to planning for emergencies is identifying potential emergency situations. This requires looking at all possible scenarios and building a comprehensive emergency plan. The plan should address situations such as floods, power outages, network outages, and system crashes.

2. Develop a Communication Plan

Once potential emergencies are identified, the next step is to develop a communication plan. This involves outlining how customer service representatives will communicate with each other during an emergency and how they will communicate with customers. Establishing communication channels and protocols can help minimize confusion and ensure everyone is on the same page.

3. Build an Emergency Response Team

Having a designated emergency response team is an essential component of effective time management in customer service. The team should consist of representatives trained to handle emergencies and equipped to respond promptly. Cross-training the team in various skills can ensure that every critical task is covered during emergencies.

4. Devise a Workflow

Representatives should have a clear workflow plan in places in case of emergencies. This involves mapping out the steps that each representative will take to resolve the issue efficiently. Creating a checklist of emergency actions will help representatives remain calm and focused in crisis situations.

5. Establish Feedback Processes

Having a feedback process in place is essential for customer service representatives to self-audit and ensure they are responding appropriately. Feedback mechanisms such as debriefings, post-emergency reports, and surveys can help identify areas for improvement and enable the team to plan better for future emergencies.

Conclusion

Planning for emergencies is essential for effective time management in customer service. Identifying potential emergencies, building teams, developing communication plans and workflows, and establishing feedback processes can help customer service teams minimize the impact of emergencies on their customers and maintain long-term relationships. A good emergency plan also supports representatives in providing prompt and efficient customer service while reassuring customers that their needs are being handled despite the unexpected situation. With proper planning, customer service representatives can ensure that they deliver excellent service in any situation.

Time management is critical in delivering excellent customer service, and setting realistic expectations is key to ensuring that representatives can manage their time effectively. Setting realistic expectations helps customer service representatives prioritize their workload, allocate their time efficiently, and ensure that they can deliver quality services to their customers. In this article, we'll discuss some strategies for setting realistic expectations and the benefits that it brings to customer service teams.

Benefits of Setting Realistic Expectations

Setting realistic expectations in customer service has several advantages, including:

1. **Clear Communication** - Clear and straightforward communication between representatives and customers helps to establish better trust, relevant information, and transparency. Set precise expectations to avoid confusion and enable customers to understand the process better.

2. **Improved Customer Experience**– Setting realistic expectations ensures customer satisfaction by providing timely and quality service. It also helps maintain honesty and integrity, which are two essential components of good customer relationships.

3. **Stress Reducing** - unrealistic expectations can lead to undue stress, anxiety, and possibly even burnout. Reps are happier, more focused, and better able to serve customers when they know what is expected of them in the time frame provided.

4. **Efficient Usage of Time** - Realistic expectations lead to time management which allows staff to plan and prioritize their workloads. This leads to time efficiency and better allocation of resources.

5. **Better Teamwork** - By setting realistic expectations, customer

service members can work collaboratively and effectively to ensure that they can manage various tasks efficiently.

Strategies for Setting Realistic Expectations

1. **Evaluate Time Frames** - Evaluate the time it takes to complete tasks and reduce processing time duration. Setting a realistic response time will prevent customer frustration with delayed responses or calls being unanswered.

2. **Know Your Limitations** - Be honest with customers about the limitations and turn-around times. Communicate when up against a busy schedule or unable to provide immediate assistance.

3. **Provide Alternatives** - Offer alternative solutions in scenarios where the customer's expectations cannot be met. This can help them better understand the situation and feel like they have been helped.

4. **Train and Develop Representatives** - Train customer service representatives to effectively manage their time and effort. Help them understand their time allocation better, and equip them with the necessary tools to be more productive.

5. **Encourage Feedback** - Regular feedback sessions can provide valuable insights into the customer's expectations and needs. Customer service teams can adjust their approach to meet customer demands and improve customer retention by taking into account sentiments gathered from customers.

Conclusion

Setting realistic expectations in customer service is essential to delivering quality service, satisfying customers, and creating positive relationships. By evaluating time frames, knowing their limitations, providing alternatives, focusing on training and development, and encouraging feedback, representatives can manage their time effectively, reduce their workload and prioritize their time efficiently to deliver proactive and consistent customer engagement. Good time management skills are vital for providing exceptional customer service, and well-managed customer support teams translate to increased satisfaction and retention rates.

Good time management is essential in customer service, as it allows representatives to prioritize their workload, deliver prompt and efficient services, and make the best possible use of the time available to them. Developing good time management habits takes time, but once mastered, it can have a significant impact on productivity, efficiency, and customer satisfaction. In this article, we'll discuss some strategies for developing good time management habits in customer service.

Start with a Clear Plan

Starting the day or shift with a clear plan of tasks to complete is the first step to good time management habits. At the beginning of each day, customer service representatives should prioritize their tasks and review what needs to be done. It helps to develop a to-do list of tasks and estimate how long it will take to complete each task. Categorize tasks according to their level of urgency, with the most urgent requiring immediate action.

Elimination of Time Wasters

Identifying and eliminating time-wasting activities is an essential part of good time management habits. Time-wasting activities can include social media, unnecessary meetings, browsing the internet, or engaging in negative conversations with coworkers. Representatives should avoid multitasking as it distracts and slows down productivity. Eliminating all distractions and staying entirely focused on their work will save time, energy and keeps them motivated.

Take Advantage of Technology

In modern times, technology has provided numerous tools that can help customer service representatives manage their time better. Various tools like Customer Relationship Management (CRM) software, time tracking software, and productivity apps are widely used to assist in time management. Take advantage of all possible technological tools to work smarter, not harder.

Integrate Smart Breaks

Taking breaks is as important as working. Integrating smart breaks will allow for better time management when implemented correctly. Continuously working for extended periods can cause the worker to burn out and make mistakes. Utilize breaks to rest, refresh and recharge. Smart breaks can include taking a brisk walk, enjoying a quick snack, or taking a stretch. This will help to avoid losing energy or focus while dealing with customers that can be demanding.

Stay Organized

Organization is vital for good time management habits. A systematic approach helps reps to access their workspace, equipment, and files quickly. A tidy environment is proven to improve workflow and can help reduce stress levels. Establishing folders, setting reminders, and utilizing a filing system categorizing clients' issues by priority can effectively manage customer service queries.

Improve Your Skills

Continuous improvement is vital to focus on good time management habits. Regular training and professional development can help identify strategies for increasing productivity and reducing workload. Build great communication and listening skills to effectively cut down on resolution time. Good time management keeps customer service professionals informed, and that education empowers them to provide better customer service.

In conclusion, good time management habits can have a significant impact on customer service teams' productivity, efficiency, and effectiveness. Starting with a clear plan, eliminating time wasters, taking advantage of technology, integrating smart breaks, staying organized, and improving skills can help customer service representatives manage their workload more effectively. Good time management habits benefit customer service agents, the organization, and customers, who benefit from timely and efficient resolution of issues.

In today's ever-changing business world, automation has made a significant impact on how organizations operate. The advancements in technology have made it possible to automate nearly everything from routine tasks, internal and external communications to customer service. With an increasing number of customer service requests coming in, automation has become essential in improving time management for customer service teams. In this article, we'll discuss some strategies for using automation to improve time management in customer service.

1. Automated Responses

Automated responses are an efficient way to acknowledge customer's requests promptly, thereby improving time management. Customers expect a quick response to their inquiries, and using automated responses can help achieve this objective. An automated response lets the customer know that their query has been received, and the team is working towards providing a solution. This effectively saves time and eliminates the need for the customer service representative to reply to each query.

2. Chatbots

Chatbots are a new trend in customer service automation that help manage customer queries with minimal human intervention. Chatbots engage customers through an instant messaging platform that simulates human conversation. It has been a significant improvement to time management in customer service, as customers can receive instant responses and continue to receive assistance outside of the working hours. Chatbots can address most common customer queries; if it is beyond their realm of knowledge, they can flag the issue for human intervention.

3. Self-service Portals

An increasingly popular form of automation is self-service portals. These portals allow customers to find solutions to their queries autonomously, saving time and effort for both customers and customer service representatives. Self-service portals can provide essential information about the product or service and frequently asked questions (FAQs), which can reduce the number of queries directed towards customer service reps.

4. Call Center Automation

Call center automation includes Interactive Voice Response (IVR) systems, automatic call distribution (ACD), and cloud-based phone systems. When a customer places a call, ACD routes calls to the appropriate department, and IVR provides them with options to choose for prompt resolution. Cloud-based phone systems allow sales and customer service teams to contact customers from anywhere, providing the flexibility needed to manage time more effectively.

5. Automated Follow-up

Automated follow-up is a powerful automation tool in customer service as it helps improve customer engagement and satisfaction levels. Automated follow-ups can include surveys, feedback collection, and offers, which can provide businesses with constructive feedback for their service delivery. It strengthens customer relationships by showing that their opinions matter and helps organizations make data-driven decisions alleviating the need for physical customer surveys.

Conclusion

Effective use of automation in customer service can significantly enhance time management as it delivers fast and accurate solutions to customer queries. Automation provides an unprecedented advantage as reps can focus on high-level tasks while automated tasks handle low-level tasks such as identification, routing, and analysis. Automated responses, chatbots, self-service portals, call center automation, and automated follow-up are just a few examples proving how useful automated processes can be in customer service. Applying the correct automation process for the right purpose can bring a competitive advantage by increasing customer satisfaction, retention rates, and overall business growth.

As a customer service representative, having problem-solving skills is crucial to your success in the field. Customer issues can be very diverse and challenging to tackle but finding ways to resolve them quickly and efficiently will ensure that customers feel satisfied, which is imperative for retaining them. In this article, we will discuss some top tips for problem-solving in a customer service environment.

1. Active Listening and Understanding

The first and most important tip is to listen and understand the issue in question. Actively listen to the customer's problem and repeat important details back to the customer to ensure that you've understood the problem correctly. This helps in clarifying the issue and indicates to the customer that their matter is important.

2. Empathy

Be empathetic towards the customer. Let the customer know that you understand their frustration and reassure them that you'll work to resolve their complaint. Empathy is key to demonstrating that you're on the customer's side and that you genuinely care about their issues.

3. Providing Solutions

Provide precise and relevant solutions to the customer. Offer a variety of solutions so the customer can pick the one that best suits their situation. Make sure that the solutions you offer solve the problem, and the customer is aware of any steps needed to implement the solution. Providing an accurate and efficient solution will increase the customer's confidence in your abilities to solve their problems.

4. Time Management

Time management is crucial when dealing with customer complaints. Ensure that you allocate appropriate time, prioritize the cases that require urgent attention, and provide quick solutions. Good time management ensures that all cases are attended to and resolved in a timely and efficient manner.

5. **Problem-Solving Approach**

Adopt a problem-solving approach to customer complaints. Try and determine the root cause of the problem, ask open-ended questions, and suggest possible solutions. Collecting information helps to build a comprehensive understanding of the issue, enabling you to address the problem more effectively, anticipate future customer complaints, and present customers with additional information to assist them.

6. **Escalation Procedures**

Have a clear escalation procedure in place in case an issue requires more advanced support or attention. Ensure that the customer understands the escalation process, and the communication channels to follow to avoid confusion or misunderstandings.

In summary, effectively handling customer complaints is a critical aspect of customer service. Active listening and understanding, empathy, providing precise solutions, good time management, a problem-solving approach, and having escalation procedures ready are all critical elements of problem-solving in a customer service environment. Incorporating these tips into your customer service approach will help in delivering an excellent customer experience, resolving complaints efficiently, and building long-term relationships with customers.

Part 10 - In Summary

To be a great customer service manager, one must focus on creating a positive and supportive work environment that motivates employees to provide excellent customer service consistently. This can be achieved by identifying individuals with the right attitude for the job, training them well, empowering them to make decisions, and creating feedback loops to monitor success. It's also important to measure customer satisfaction and make necessary changes to improve overall customer service. A great customer service manager must prioritize their customers' needs, build relationships with them, and go above and beyond to exceed their expectations. Communication skills, problem-solving abilities, and attention to detail are just a few of the essential qualities required to be a successful customer service manager.

Appendix – I

Great Leaders In History

Need some inspiration? Many prominent figures throughout history have exemplified great leadership characteristics. Here are some noteworthy examples of historical leaders:

1. **Mahatma Gandhi**: Gandhi was a famous Indian leader whose principles of peaceful resistance and civil disobedience led India to independence from British rule. He is known for inspiring people with his humble and compassionate nature and his dedication to non-violent action.

2. **Nelson Mandela**: Mandela was a South African anti-apartheid leader who became the country's first black president. He spent 27 years in prison for his struggle against apartheid, where he became a symbol of resilience and forgiveness.

3. **Abraham Lincoln**: Lincoln was the 16th President of the United States of America. His leadership helped the country reunite in the aftermath of the Civil War and end slavery through the Emancipation Proclamation.

4. **Winston Churchill**: Churchill was a British Prime Minister whose leadership during World War II is widely viewed as his defining moment. He rallied the British people to keep fighting even in the face of defeat, inspiring courage and perseverance in his countrymen.

5. **Martin Luther King Jr.**: King was an American Baptist minister who became the most prominent leader of the American Civil Rights Movement. He is known for his advocacy of non-violent resistance to promote racial equality and his famous "I Have a Dream" speech.

6. **Julius Caesar**: Caesar was a Roman general and statesman who played a significant role in the rise of the Roman Empire. His military strategy, political acumen, and leadership skills contributed to his success and helped shape the modern world.

7. **Alexander the Great:** Alexander was a king of Macedonia who conquered a vast empire that stretched from Greece to India. He is known for his military leadership, strategic vision, and commitment to promoting Greek culture throughout his empire.

These great leaders are remembered not only for their accomplishments, but also for their exemplary leadership qualities. They inspire individuals to strive for greatness and make a positive impact on others.

Mahatma Gandhi

Mahatma Gandhi was an Indian nationalist leader who is revered for his non-violent civil disobedience movement against British colonial rule in India. His leadership style was unique, inspired and transformative for his time. Here are some key characteristics of Gandhi's leadership style:

1. **Non-Violence**

Gandhi's leadership style was rooted in the philosophy of non-violence. He believed that violence only begets more violence and that any change must be peaceful.

2. **Empathy**

Gandhi was empathetic to the needs and sufferings of ordinary people. He believed that coming down to their level of consciousness and understanding their thoughts and feelings were necessary to direct and motivate them.

3. **Lead from the front**

Gandhi led by example. He practiced what he preached and always remained committed to his principles.

4. **Simplicity**

Gandhi was known for his simplicity - both in his way of life and in his communication. He was always willing to listen to others and meet them where they were.

5. Selflessness

Gandhi led a life of service to others. He emphasized the need for personal sacrifice for the greater cause of social or political change.

6. Courage

Gandhi's leadership style was characterized by his extraordinary courage. He had the courage to stand up for what he believed in, no matter how difficult or dangerous the situation was.

7. Self-Reflection

Gandhi believed in self-reflection as part of leadership. He took time to introspect and understand his own limitations, strengths and weaknesses.

Overall, Gandhi's leadership style was unique, inspired and transformative for his time. His philosophy of non-violence, empathy, simplicity, selflessness, courage, and self-reflection have influenced civil rights leaders across the world. Gandhi believed that leading by example and being committed to one's principles was the key to transformative leadership.

Nelson Mandela

Nelson Mandela is considered to be one of the most inspirational leaders of the 20th century. He was a South African anti-apartheid revolutionary, who fought against racial discrimination and inequality. His leadership style was characterized by his sense of justice, his ability to inspire, his resilience, and his diplomatic approach. Here are some key characteristics of Mandela's leadership style:

1. Visionary

Mandela had a clear vision for a free and democratic South Africa, where all citizens could live in equality and peace. He was able to articulate this vision to his followers, inspiring them to work towards a better future.

2. Inclusive

Mandela was known for his inclusive approach to leadership. He believed in bringing people of different backgrounds and perspectives together to work towards a common goal.

3. Resilient

Mandela spent 27 years in prison for his beliefs, but remained steadfast in his principles and his commitment to justice. He emerged from prison even more committed to his cause and continued to fight for change.

4. **Diplomatic**

Mandela understood the importance of diplomacy and negotiation in achieving his goals. He was a skilled negotiator who was able to bring together disparate groups and find common ground.

5. **Inspirational**

Mandela was able to inspire his followers through his words and his example. He was a gifted speaker who could rally his supporters and motivate them to take action.

6. **Humility**

Despite his many accomplishments, Mandela remained humble and focused on his mission. He was able to connect with people on a personal level and show empathy for their struggles.

Overall, Mandela's leadership style was characterized by his sense of justice, his ability to inspire, his resilience, his diplomatic approach, his inclusiveness, and his humility. These qualities helped him to achieve remarkable changes in South Africa and inspire people all over the world.

Abraham Lincoln

Abraham Lincoln was one of the greatest leaders in American history, renowned for his exceptional leadership style. As a President during one of the most challenging times in US history, he had an enormous responsibility to preserve the Union and fight for civil rights. Lincoln's leadership approach was characterized by his humility, integrity, vision, and his ability to inspire and empower others. In this article, we will discuss Abraham Lincoln's leadership style.

1. **Humility**

Lincoln's humility was one of his most distinguishable traits. He never pretended to know everything or have all the answers, and he was always willing to listen to other people's perspectives. He acknowledged his mistakes and used them as learning opportunities, which made him relatable and trustworthy.

2. **Visionary**

Lincoln had a clear and inspiring vision for America. He believed in the importance of the Union and democracy, as well as equal rights for everyone. He created a country where all Americans had the opportunity to achieve their full potential, irrespective of their background or status.

3. Empowering

Lincoln empowered his team and believed in their abilities. He delegated important roles and tasks to his Cabinet members and trusted them to deliver results. He knew that working together as a team was critical to achieving the common goal.

4. Communicative

Lincoln was an excellent communicator, who used his words to inspire and unite his countrymen. He was a gifted speaker and writer, who knew just how to deliver the right words that could ignite a spark in the hearts of his audience. His speeches, including the Gettysburg Address and second inaugural address, are still celebrated today.

5. Integrity

Lincoln's integrity and moral character were legendary. He always stood for what he believed was right, even when it was unpopular. His actions were guided by strong ethical principles, and he would never compromise on his beliefs or values, even at great personal cost.

In conclusion, Abraham Lincoln's leadership style was characterized by his humility, vision, empowerment, communication, and integrity. He knew what needed to be done for the betterment of his country, and he was not afraid to face any extraordinary challenges along the way to inspire his team and achieve their goals. Lincoln's leadership remains a source of inspiration to current and future generations of leaders.

Winston Churchill

Winston Churchill was one of the most prominent and successful leaders of the 20th century. His leadership style was characterized by his ability to inspire, his clear vision, his strategic thinking, and his decisive action. Here are some key characteristics of Churchill's leadership style:

1. Inspirational Communication

Churchill was a highly skilled public speaker who used his speeches to rally his people and inspire them to fight against difficult odds. His speeches were known for their emotional impact, wit, and eloquence.

2. Decisiveness

Churchill had a reputation for making quick, tough decisions. During World War II, he was known for his ability to make important strategic decisions and take decisive military action.

3. High Expectations

Churchill expected a lot from his subordinates and held them to high standards of performance. He was known for being demanding and setting high expectations for himself as well.

4. Strategic Thinking

Churchill had a keen sense of strategy and a deep understanding of the geopolitical landscape of his time. He was able to develop effective strategies for winning World War II and shaping post-war Europe.

5. Resilience

Churchill faced many setbacks and challenges in his career, but he remained committed to his vision and demonstrated resilience in the face of adversity. His leadership style reflected his ability to persevere in the face of difficulties and maintain a long-term perspective.

6. A sense of history

Churchill had a deep appreciation for history and saw himself as part of a long tradition of European leadership. He brought a sense of historical perspective to his decision-making and was able to learn from past mistakes and successes.

Overall, Churchill's leadership style was characterized by his ability to inspire, his strategic thinking and decisiveness, his high expectations, and his resilience in the face of adversity. These qualities helped him shape history and cement his legacy as one of the greatest leaders of the 20th century.

Martin Luther King Jr

Martin Luther King Jr. was an iconic civil rights leader who championed for freedom, equality, and justice for all. His leadership style was transformative, inspiring, and powerful, as he brought together millions of people to work together towards a common vision. Dr. King was a trailblazer, who led by example and inspired people to find the courage to stand up for what they believed in. In this article, we will explore Martin Luther King Jr's leadership style.

1. Leading by Example

Dr. King's leadership style centered around leading by example. He used his speech, his writing, his peaceful protests, and his life to show people that it was possible to change societal injustice through peaceful means. His commitment to the cause was evident to all and inspired people to follow.

2. Emphasizing the Importance of Non-violent Resistance

Dr. King advocated for non-violent resistance as a means of effecting change. This approach empowered people to use their civil rights to fight against injustice without resorting to violent means. He believed that nonviolence offered a moral high ground that could win hearts and minds.

3. Articulating the Cause

Dr. King had a unique ability to articulate the cause of civil rights to the American public. He used his speeches to create unified vision, one that resonated with the masses. Through clear articulation of a vision, he galvanized people to join the civil rights movement.

4. Collaborative

Dr. King believed that collaboration was key to achieving success in any civil rights campaign. He worked closely with his team of advisors, always seeking their diverse opinions. He also worked with other leaders, including religious leaders and political leaders, to create a unified message to bring people together.

5. **Visionary**

Dr. King was a true visionary, with a clear idea of what he wanted for his country. He believed in the cause he fought for, and his vision for a better America was the driving force behind his work.

In conclusion, Martin Luther King Jr's leadership style was centered around leading by example, emphasizing the importance of non-violent resistance, articulating the cause of civil rights, being collaborative and visionary. He is a model of exemplary leadership, who inspired millions of people to work towards a common goal. Dr. King's legacy endures, inspiring current and future generations of leaders to work towards a just society.

Julius Caesar

Julius Caesar was one of the most successful military generals and statesmen in Roman history, known for his exceptional leadership style. Caesar's leadership was notable for his ability to inspire and motivate his soldiers, his tactical intelligence, and his political acumen. In this article, we will explore the key elements of Julius Caesar's leadership style.

1. Confidence and Courage

Caesar had a remarkable level of confidence and courage that inspired his soldiers in times of battle. He was known for fighting alongside his troops, and his willingness to lead from the front enhanced their confidence in his leadership abilities. Caesar never hesitated to take calculated risks, and his courage spurred his troops to do the same.

2. Charisma and Eloquence

Another critical element of Julius Caesar's leadership style was his charismatic personality and eloquence of speech. Caesar had a natural ability to connect with people, and his speeches were incredibly persuasive, inspiring loyalty and support. He understood the power of public speaking and used it to his advantage.

3. Strategic Thinking

Caesar was an astute strategist and tactician. He was able to accurately assess situations, anticipate challenges, and formulate practical solutions. He was known to be an agile thinker and a quick learner, adapting to changing circumstances with ease.

4. Decisiveness

Caesar was known for his decisiveness, which was instrumental in his success as a military leader. He could make quick decisions based on the information available and act without hesitation. He had the ability to capitalize on opportunities presented to him, and his quick and decisive actions often caught his enemies off-guard.

5. Discipline and Order

Caesar believed in maintaining discipline and order in his troops, and he insisted on strict obedience to the chain of command. He ensured that his soldiers adhered to a strict code of conduct, which helped in maintaining high morale, reducing tension and increasing productivity.

In conclusion, Julius Caesar's leadership style was characterized by his confidence, courage, charisma, strategic thinking, decisiveness, and discipline. He had a remarkable ability to inspire and motivate his troops, and his tactical genius and political acumen enabled him to achieve success both in the battlefield and at the political front. Caesar's leadership style remains an inspiration to this day, and his legacy continues to influence leadership models worldwide.

Alexander The Great

Alexander the Great was a legendary leader who conquered much of the ancient world. His leadership style was characterized by his ability to inspire loyalty, his strategic vision, his military genius, and his daring nature. Here are some key characteristics of Alexander's leadership style:

1. Vision

Alexander had a clear vision of what he wanted to achieve - to unite the peoples of the world under one empire. He was able to articulate this vision to his troops, inspiring them to follow him into battle.

2. Military Genius

Alexander was a brilliant military strategist and tactician. He was able to outmaneuver and defeat much larger armies, thanks to his ability to read the terrain, to surprise his opponents, and to use tactics that exploited his enemies' weaknesses.

3. People Skills

Despite his fearsome reputation as a warrior and conqueror, Alexander was also an excellent people person. He was quick to recognize talent in others and to reward it. He was also able to inspire loyalty in his troops, who were often willing to fight to the death for him.

4. **Daring**

Alexander was known for his audacious plans and his willingness to take risks. He often put himself in danger alongside his troops and was always at the front line of battle. This daring nature helped inspire his troops and demoralize his enemies.

5. **Adaptability**

Alexander was able to adapt to changing circumstances and to think on his feet. This helped him navigate complex situations and to improvise when things didn't go according to plan.

Overall, Alexander's leadership style was characterized by his ability to inspire, his strategic vision, his military genius, his daring nature, and his adaptability. These qualities helped him conquer much of the ancient world and leave a lasting impact on history.